FROM UTOPIA TO NIGHTMARE

SLC

FROM UTOPIA
TO NIGHTMARE

by
CHAD WALSH

GREENWOOD PRESS, PUBLISHERS
WESTPORT, CONNECTICUT

Library of Congress Cataloging in Publication Data

Walsh, Chad, 1914-
    From Utopia to nightmare.

    Bibliography: p.
    1. Utopias--History. I. Title.
[HX806.W2 1972]   321'.07   71-38130
ISBN 0-8371-6325-0

Originally published in 1962 by Harper & Row, Publishers,
New York

Reprinted with the permission of Harper & Row, Publishers

Reprinted by Greenwood Press, Inc.

First Greenwood reprinting 1972
Second Greenwood reprinting 1975
Third Greenwood reprinting 1977

Library of Congress catalog card number 71-38130

ISBN 0-8371-6325-0

Printed in the United States of America

For Joseph Fletcher

Acknowledgements

AN EXTRAORDINARY number of people had a helpful hand in the writing of this book and I take this opportunity to express my gratitude, though there is not space to list all of them by name.

First of all, my thanks to my wife, Eva, who scanned a vast number of novels, most of which she cordially detested, to see which ones fell within the scope of my study and required my attention.

Secondly, a brief inquiry that I published in the book review of *The New York Times* resulted in nearly a hundred letters, many of which mentioned books useful for my purpose, or contained interesting observations on utopia and dystopia. To this widely scattered brotherhood of utopian and dystopian connoisseurs, my thanks.

During the academic year 1960–1 I taught an honours seminar in 'Utopia and Anti-Utopia' at Beloit College and my students, through their class discussion and papers, stimulated me and gave me more insights than they could realise. Let me thank them by name: Charlene Ruth Becker, Fredrica Beth Beyerman, Richard A. Fineberg, Marshall Fraser, Charles F. Grose, Fred Hopman, Sue H. Longley, Richard Lower, Sharon Ruhl, Joan Sandquist, Linda M. Treat, Virginia VanWart Gage, Susan Wright.

My thanks also to the always obliging and co-operative staff of the Beloit College Libraries.

And special thanks to two scholars: Prof. J. Max Patrick

kindly put his vast background of utopian and dystopian learning at my service by reading and criticising the manuscript: the book is a better one for his generous concern. Another scholar, my good friend the Reverend Professor Joseph Fletcher of Episcopal Theological School, devoted many hours to a minute examination of the original lectures from which this book evolved. Though he will still not agree with all my conclusions, he will recognise his influence in many passages that we debated together in his study. As a token of my appreciation, I have dedicated the work to him.

I have, of course, made reference to a great many works and quoted briefly from many of them. For permission to reprint longer passages I am indebted to Messrs. Faber & Faber of London and Random House Inc., of New York for rights in the poem 'The Unknown Citizen' from *Collected Shorter Poems* by W. H. Auden and to Messrs. E. P. Dutton & Co. Inc., of New York for rights in *We* by Eugene Zamiatin, translated by Dr. Gregory Zilboorg.

Finally, any book of this sort leans heavily on the pioneer work done by other scholars. In the appendix I have listed a few of the books I found most useful. All of them lightened my task.

1962   C. W.

Contents

Preface

A FEW YEARS ago the Episcopal Theological School of Cambridge, Massachusetts, invited me to give the annual Kellogg Lectures to the faculty, students and alumni. This distinguished lectureship, honouring the memory of the Reverend Frederic Brainerd Kellogg and his father, Frederic Rogers Kellogg, is often devoted to exploring some theological frontier, in particular the interrelation of theology and other disciplines.

For my topic I proposed a subject to which I had already devoted considerable thought and speculation: the gradual decline in our times of the utopian novel and its displacement by the 'dystopia' or 'inverted utopia'. It seemed to me that this shift in literary fashion must have a significance more than literary. If alert readers once sat down with Bellamy's *Looking Backward* or Wells's *A Modern Utopia* and today seem more likely to meditate upon Huxley's *Brave New World* or Orwell's *Nineteen Eighty-Four*, this surely points to important changes in that no-man's-land where literature, sociology, psychology, political science, theology and philosophy meet without clear boundaries. In short, I hoped by examining the decline of one sort of book and the rise of its apparent opposite to learn something about the condition of modern man and his society.

Stimulated by the invitation from the ETS and the categorical imperative of a deadline, I intensified my researches through what is a literary jungle, among books many of which are out of print and scarcely known to the standard literary scholar. The result was four lectures that I

11

delivered in 1959. I profited greatly from meeting interested, keen and critical minds in the give-and-take of debate after-wards. I saw that I needed to do still more reading and thinking before I offered the lectures for publication. Hence the delay.

The present book is about twice as long as the original lectures, and for the reader's convenience is divided into conventional chapters. I have not, however, tried to convert lectures into formal essays. The tone of the speaking voice remains. All current allusions have been 'updated' (as of early 1962).

From Utopia to Nightmare makes no pretence of being a definitive study of the inverted utopia. That formidable book remains to be written by someone with more patience than I have. My purpose was highly selective. I simply chose those stories — mainly 19th and 20th century — that seemed in their dystopian way to be saying something im-portant about the human condition. I studied and analysed them to discern their significance. I tried always to see them against their historical and ideological background.

The sociologist or political scientist who chances on this book may find too much religion for his special interests. The theologian will think he is reading a treatise on sociology and political science. The literary critic will wonder how many of these books are worth the time it takes to read them. For all this, I have no apologies. There is much talk about the breakdown of communication between specialists in the various disciplines. *From Utopia to Nightmare* is one small attempt, by a writer who is a layman in all but two of the relevant disciplines, to examine a peculiar body of literature and show that its insights and implications are simul-taneously literary, sociological, political, psychological, philosophic, ethical, and religious.

Beloit College   Chad Walsh

CHAPTER ONE

The Waning of Utopia

THE WARS and revolutionary upheavals of the past half-century have erased many names from the map. The Austro-Hungarian Empire exists only in history books and memories of the ageing; Montenegro is now part of Jugoslavia; the Baltic States — Lithuania, Estonia, and Latvia — have disappeared in silence behind the Iron Curtain and barely survive as diplomatic wraiths. Meanwhile new nations with names like Viet-Nam, Ghana, and the Republic of Upper Volta appear in proud, bright splashes on the map.

There is another change, perhaps as important as those I have mentioned. In the midst of old countries disappearing and new ones coming to birth, few men have paused to notice that a familiar and cherished nation, unique in offering honorary citizenship to all humanity, is in danger of quietly fading from the map. That country is Utopia. Its name is supposed to mean 'nowhere', but for centuries it has emphatically been somewhere. It has loomed larger on the map of human spirit and imagination than most of the nations whose deeds and misdeeds fill the airwaves and provoke special sessions of the U.N. General Assembly.

During this century there has been an unequalled production of imaginary societies. Some have appeared in hard covers. Many are born and die between the lurid covers of science-fiction magazines or paperbacks. Any reader can flee from his daily round of work and sober domesticity by reading his way to a remote island, a Himalayan valley, the centre of the earth; to times future, times outside the conventional stream of time; to Mars or Venus or planets so remote they can be reached only by a space-warp. And arriving at any of these destinations, he can find practically any type of society that his imagination yearns for. But the significant fact is this. A decreasing percentage of the imaginary worlds are utopias. An increasing percentage are nightmares. The 'dystopia' or 'inverted utopia' or 'anti-utopia' — I shall use the terms interchangeably — was a minor satiric fringe of the utopian output in the 19th century. It promises to become the dominant type today, if it has not already achieved statistical preponderance.

It is not that the writing of utopias has ceased. Prof. B. F. Skinner of the Harvard Psychology Department published an impressive utopia, *Walden Two*, in 1948, delineating a community kept happy and co-operative by the ministrations of a panel of psychologists. Aldous Huxley, to the surprise of his admirers, recently published a *bona fide* utopia, *Island*. By a little hunting, you can find other recent or fairly recent utopias that command some degree of intellectual respect. But for the most part, the utopias being offered today are class C. They usually lack a comprehensive, clear-eyed vision of society as a whole. Many of them are quaint and crotchety. An ex-G.I. named Albert Archer Van Petten in *The Great Man's Life* 1925 *to* 2000 *A. C.* has set out to demonstrate that world bliss would ensue if mankind took the principle of contract seriously. For instance, the couple contemplating marriage can work out their own arrangements — monogamous or plural, or perhaps a five-year contract of matrimony with option of renewal upon mutual satisfaction. H. L. Hunt, the Texas oil magnate, has privately published *Alpaca*, a romance which alternates between the adventures of a hero and heroine (who shivers deliciously at his presence) and the creation of a new constitution for imaginary Alpaca. This latter includes such novelties as a 25 per cent limitation on the income tax, a provision that people who pay higher taxes get extra ballots, and a permanent committee to investigate the loyalty of government employees. To every man his own utopia.

'A map of the world that does not include Utopia is not worth even glancing at, for it leaves out the one country at which Humanity is always landing,' Oscar Wilde wrote. He died in 1900. The reader looking for current utopias is likely to find them bumbling and unconvincing. But if he wants expertly-presented nightmares, he can choose among a greater variety of horrors than Dante on his pilgrimage through the nine circles of hell.

The decline of utopia and the rise of its nightmare cousin is parallel to the history of this surrealist century, which is at once the partial fulfilment of 19th-century dreams and their negation. The old hope of steady progress, one grants, has been crowned by many concrete achievements, and further ones are possible. Atomic energy *could* produce a paradise of abundance with a minimum of sweat and exploitation. The United Nations *could* become the Parliament of Man. The physicians have almost conquered polio. Lives, when not abruptly terminated, are longer. Education is spreading. Racial prejudice is slowly eroding in many places. The achievements of the 20th century are not negligible. A 19th-century *revenant* might at first smile happily, seeing before him the land of his heart's desire.

And yet, it would take him only a few minutes with the daily newspaper and a few hours with a modern history book to discover that progress has worn a double face. Atomic energy has made few deserts blossom, but it has made two cities wither. The United Nations often behave, in the words of President de Gaulle, like the Disunited Nations. Longevity increases; so does the profession of geriatrics; so does the pressure of an exploding world population against the resources of a globe only trivially enlarged each year by meteoric dust. Most of all, the *revenant* from the 19th century would learn that the dream of enduring peace — a plausible and rational hope in the interlude between Napoleon and 1914 — had been interrupted by two world wars and is now threatened by a third, and that the sane march towards democratic and liberal institutions throughout the world has been diverted or perverted by men wearing black shirts, brown shirts, red shirts — or sometimes stiff white shirts.

Thus the 20th century wears its double face. The question is no longer whether a rational and abundant society is technically feasible, but whether men are capable of the rationality and goodness to create and sustain it. Our century, then, has been forced to look more closely than did our grandfathers at the human raw material of which utopia must be constructed. The verdict is not yet officially rendered, but rumours from the jury-room are not encouraging.

It is true that the dream of inevitable progress dies hard. The occasional utopias still written testify to its persistence. It lingers on also in a good deal of political oratory, and in the half-unconscious assumptions of millions, Americans in particular, who are still prone to hail the latest thing — whether the U.N. or a presidential victory or some scientific break-through — as the prelude to the bright, clean world of the future. In its ghostly way, utopia continues to haunt mankind. It is a good ghost that won't go away. In the same fashion, refugees from the Baltic states keep Estonia, Lithuania and Latvia alive in their faithful hearts, and give to these vanished nations a kind of metaphysical endurance, no matter what little splashes of colour have been erased from the map.

The Waning of Utopia

Now that I have said all this, I must return to the incontrovertible point that most 20th-century writers who care to speculate about possible societies seem to have lost their utopian dreams. (I am speaking of writers this side of the Iron Curtain. Soviet utopianism is a special case which I shall discuss later.) I regard this as a fact sufficiently arresting to deserve attention. Granted that writers do not have a sixth sense denied to less sensitive mortals; they are not infallible soothsayers and prophets; they can lose their all on the stock market as quickly as their banker neighbours, and make marriages as catastrophic as those of millionaire playboys. Grant all this — writers are still very often the most accurate barometers we have. Sometimes their accuracy of detail almost convinces the reader that they have indeed peered into a crystal ball. Glancing through Ignatius Donnelly's *Caesar's Column*, a novel of the future published in 1892, you quickly discover that it predicts for the 20th century such things as: aeroplanes, TV, poison gas, the 'cell' methods of political organisation, racial uprisings, genocide, a common denominator religion in the schools, the welfare state, abolition of the gold standard, a National Health Service of socialised medicine, the 8-hour 5-day week. In fact, the book predicts very few things that have not come to pass in one place or another.

I do not wish to press the point too far. Writers are often very wide of the mark in their specific prophecies of the future. I would not argue that one should turn to them to learn what milady will be wearing in the year 2000, but to get a foretaste of the attitudes that will shape the future. When I first began teaching T. S. Eliot's *The Waste Land*, the ideas and moods were so alien to my students that I felt like an anthropologist trying to help his class enter sympathetically into the tabu system of some tribe that only anthropologists had visited. Today it is easier going. The radical

pessimism and faint gleams of hope, hope in spite of everything, that *The Waste Land* brokenly but powerfully con-
veys, seem to tally with the way my students feel. Even the
mythological way of saying things is much easier for them
than formerly. Many of them have already bid good-bye to
any sunny rationalism and have gone off Zen-ward or into
the luminous absurdities of Existentialism.

Now there is a problem here. Did Eliot and other writers
create a new sensibility which gradually penetrated the reasonably literate world, so that today's students are more at
home with *The Waste Land* simply because the poem has —
at second or third remove —taught them how to experience
the century? Or was Eliot, when he wrote the poem, simply
a person with unusually sensitive antennae? Did he sense the
psychological shape of things to come, so that in depicting a
particular mood he was not creating it but describing it in
advance?

It must surely be something of both. Sometimes the influence of an author is obvious and direct. Bacon's description of Solomon's House in *The New Atlantis* helped to
inspire the founding of the Royal Society and its early
researches. Usually the influence is less direct. *Avant-garde* art
teaches its technical tricks to those artists who prepare advertisements in the glossier magazines; eventually the lowly
cereal package shows the trace of modernity. The most advanced pronouncements from the seminaries reach the
ordinary pulpit half a generation later, and still later become
the sterile, commonsense assumptions of the normal church-
goer. The novelists were tearing the fabric of Victorian
morality into little bits for successive decades before the
Flaming Twenties flamed up in revolt against the deceased
queen. In all these instances, advanced minds and sensibilities helped to create a new climate of opinion and attitude.
There has been a trickle-down and permeation.

The Waning of Utopia

Any powerful mind, expressing itself in any public way, is a shaper of the next period. But even more important, or so I suspect, is the second process. Perhaps the writer, if I may centre attention on him, does not so much create the attitudes of the next generation and their sensibility, as sense them. He lives a little ahead of his time. Thomas Hardy helped in a small way to topple the Victorian moral edifice, but it was already crumbling behind the façade, though few were aware of this. He had eyes of vision. He could look at the façade and see both its impressive outline and the future ruins. He lived simultaneously in his own period and in the new period that was to come. The change would have come to pass, Hardy or no Hardy. But because he saw it and described it, it came a little more rapidly and surely.

What I have been saying applies also to many of the advances of science. Medieval man must have sometimes come on a fossil when he dug the foundations for cathedral or castle, and there is no reason why he should not have speculated and arrived at some theory of the earth's great age and the evolution of life. No reason, except that it wasn't 'in the air'. It was easier and more natural and 'reasonable' to dismiss the strange objects as meaningless freaks or relics of the Flood. On the other hand, the idea of evolution did not spring fullblown from Darwin's brain. He had been preceded by Lamarck and also by Tennyson. The poet, though no habitué of the laboratories, was aware of the earth's antiquity, the rise and fall of species, the impersonal cruelty of nature, the struggle for survival. His *In Memoriam*, where all this is expressed, is earlier than *The Origin of Species*. Darwin came along at the right time. The idea of evolution was in the air. It was easy to think evolutionary thoughts, to express them, to be understood. Most people, it is true, were still more at home with Archbishop Ussher's chronology than with Darwin's, and the opposition — ecclesiastical and

scientific — was bitter. But Darwin, with his precise state-
ment of an idea that was vaguely everywhere among the
more perceptive, was the intellectual wave of the future.
Thus his theory won rapid acceptance from most of the
people who counted. And again, by formulating the idea in
its classic form, he made the wave of the future move a little
faster.

The same sensitivity, the same ability to perceive slight
tremors in the air and give them objective expression before
the average person is aware of them, is seen in the various
arts. During the late 19th and early 20th century painting,
sculpture and music began mutating into such new forms
that an 18th-century connoisseur would be both affronted
and mystified in the better modern museums and concert
halls. In music, classical tonality was deliberately forsaken by
many of the most gifted composers. In painting and sculpture, some artists have gone off in surrealist exploitation of
the subconscious, while others have abandoned any pretence to external objectivity and have created abstractions
that depict, perhaps, spiritual and psychological facts, but
nothing remotely photographable. The old aesthetic assumptions have burst asunder and into fragments; a new
'vocabulary' is in process of creation. To the average person, if not to the artist, the result sometimes appears to be
nightmare chaos. But isn't 'nightmare chaos' a good, brief
description of the world since 1914? The world wars, the
mass bombings, the nuclear bombs, the spread of rival
totalitarianisms, the concentration camps, the extermination
camps, lamps made of human parchment, gold extracted
from the teeth of corpses, the perfection of brainwashing as
the latest of the fine arts — who in the moderately sunny
19th century would have predicted all these things? Who
would have foretold that two great world-powers would
have the capacity to destroy not merely each other, but all

mankind, and that the continuance of the race would depend on the rationality of two lonely men?

The arts, in their strange mutations from norms that had seemed as stable and obvious as the Golden Rule, foreshadowed the shape of things to come. They proclaimed by the bizarre violence of their mutations that the old order was far frailer than men thought and that strange figures were stalking at the fringes of civil society, ready to lunge and take over—or annihilate.

All this is by way of prologue to explain why, quite apart from literary and aesthetic considerations, we must take the writers seriously. What they are thinking and feeling and fearing today may be the way your children, and the children of the man in the street, will think, feel, and fear tomorrow.

If the utopian vision is no longer able to fire the imagination of many first-rate writers, if the future appears to them more as a tale told by an idiot than a saga of rational achievement, this may not indicate a deplorable failure of nerve on the writer's part. Perhaps he just happens to have a keen and agonized insight into the way history is moving.

You may not agree with what I have just said. But you will surely agree that the brute *fact* of the shift — the decline in utopian writing and the rise of the inverted utopia — is a startling thing, and deserves a careful second glance. Perhaps it has important social, philosophic, and religious implications. If so, we want to know what they are. They may have to do with our welfare, our very survival.

At this point I suspect some of you are tempted to rejoice. Utopia is waning; that sounds good. Utopia has received rather a bad press in the inner circles of Christendom, at least since the rise of Neo-Orthodoxy and its stern reaction against the sunny and sometimes soft optimism of the old Social Gospel. Even though the book that gave us

21

the word utopia was written by a man who died a martyr
for his faith and bears the title of saint, the suspicion lingers
that the utopian impulse is purely humanistic; that it represents a further stage of that primal rebellion of Adam and
Eve. Like them, the utopian wants mankind to have 'a life
of its own', to shape its own destiny without too much regard to any Creator and the fact of creaturehood. Perhaps
utopia is a blasphemous attempt to deprive the angels of
their flaming swords and batter our way back into paradise.

This suspicion of utopia and utopians is partially justified,
as I hope to show later. The utopias vary greatly in the role
they assign to God, but in general the hope of an earthly
utopia can exist at all only because the dreamer assumes that
he and his neighbours are good enough and rational enough
to sit down and plan a better world. Not merely plan it, but
build it.

Such an attitude may or may not be presumption and
hubris, depending on definitions and the spirit in which the
utopian enterprise is undertaken. I grant that some degree of
Christian suspicion and reserve is justified. Utopian credentials need careful study in each separate case. The Christian
will usually wish to add some provisos and footnotes. But
at the same time, let me suggest that any premature re-
joicing over the disappearance of utopia from the map of
man's spirit runs the danger of revealing more Christian
Schadenfreude then Christian charity. In the theological
counter-revolution against the liberalism of our fathers,
there has been an inevitable swing to the opposite extreme.
Our temptation now is not to over-rate man but to gloat
with twitching nostrils over each evidence of his finitude
and nastiness. In some theological circles I am more vividly
aware of Original Sin than of its remedy.

Theoretically, the loss of utopian hopes could mean
simply that man is abandoning his humanistic delusions and

returning to Christian realism. But it can equally well mean that a mood of total pessimism, as unreasoned as the earlier utopian hopes, is engulfing our minds and our spirits. The decline of utopianism does not mark a clear gain in Christian perspectives. Rather, like all changes, it simply poses a new set of questions. The deepening pessimism of our century (again speaking of this side of the Iron Curtain) is a fact. In itself it is not a retreat from Christianity or an advance towards it. The Christian is challenged to understand it, to find his way through it and perhaps beyond it.

But before spending too much time on the religious dimensions of what is, narrowly conceived, a shift in literary taste, it will be necessary to take a very swift backward look at the utopian tradition, out of which the dystopian reaction has sprung. And before utopia can be briefly explored, we must first define our terms.

CHAPTER TWO

Dreams, Nightmares and Definitions

LET ME make clear what I hope to do and — equally important — what I make no pretence of doing. My thesis is that, to judge by the output and quality of books dealing with imaginary societies, the utopian hope is declining and being replaced by nightmarish apprehensions. I think this is a striking fact. It is of some literary importance, and may be of still more sociological, psychological, philosophic and religious significance.

My focus will be on dystopia. I shall deal with utopia only briefly, as a necessary background to its mocking rival.

Now for definitions. Webster says under Utopia:

A book (1516) by Sir Thomas More, describing an ideal commonwealth. Utopia is an imaginary island, enjoying perfection in politics, law, etc. Hence, any place of ideal perfection; also, an impractical scheme of social regeneration.

We may disregard the pejorative sense of utopia — 'an impractical scheme of social regeneration'. It is found on the lips of Niebuhrians, who suspect a Pelagian naïveté in all utopian blueprints; it is also employed by two groups that seemingly have little in common: diehard conservatives who date the downfall of any country from its introduction of income tax, and doctrinaire Marxists intent on demolishing the non-Marxist socialist thought of the 19th century.

My concern is with utopia as utopians understand the word. 'An ideal commonwealth . . . enjoying perfection in politics, law, etc.' This brings out the pun in the word. *Utopia* comes from two Greek words meaning 'no place.' But the word would still be pronounced the same in English if written *eutopia*, which would mean 'good place'. More apparently intended the double meaning — a good place which is no place.

For my purposes, however, I find the noun 'perfection' too limiting. Many books which I — and probably the utopians themselves — would unhesitatingly call utopias do not present a perfect society, but simply one better than society as we actually observe it. H. G. Wells's *A Modern Utopia* is an example at hand. It still has its ne'er-do-wells, its drunkards and dope addicts. Yet it is a world considerably more rational and humane than the one we inhabit, and its momentum is towards a still closer approach to perfection, though Wells does not imply that the goal will ever be absolutely attained.

Let me modify the Webster definition by stretching the word utopia to include not merely an ideal or perfect society, but also any imaginary society presented as superior to the actual world. If the society is still evolving and moving towards clear and desirable ends, its claim to the title is that much stronger.

This brings up one minor point to be clarified. The intent of an author is crucial. I have heard an occasional college student say he wished he could live in Aldous Huxley's *Brave New World*, and I do not doubt the sincerity of his desire. The student's comment proves not that Mr. Huxley was writing a utopia but rather that the student was an imperceptive reader. Anyone skimming through *Brave New World* with a bare minimum of literary acumen will know after twenty pages that the author loathes this idiotically happy world of feelies, Malthusian belts, and prenatal happiness-engineering. *Brave New World* is not a utopia but a dystopia. Always, a writer's intention is what counts. It is up to the reader to read between the lines and discern that intention.

To take a reverse situation, *Walden Two* depicts a world so repulsive to me that I should like to think it was intended as a dystopia. But I know it isn't. Prof. Skinner is plainly out to present an ideal world, from his point of view.* I must accept his intention. He intends *Walden Two* as a utopia; a utopia it is.

Returning now to the definition of utopia, a rough approximation might be 'an imaginary society presented as superior to any society that actually exists'. An inverted utopia would be the opposite — 'an imaginary society presented as inferior to any civilised society that actually exists.' In each case, one could refine the definition by making it clear that the writer may be thinking only of familiar societies when he makes his comparisons. He might write a utopia picturing a world better than his own, without knowing that somewhere in the jungles of New Guinea there was a still more utopian flesh-and-blood society. But this is a minor and highly theoretical consideration.

A utopia is often an oblique satire on the writer's own society, though it need not be. It can represent simply his attempt to conceive of a perfect society, without regard to the merits and defects of his own. An inverted utopia, in its turn, is often a deliberate attack on the idea and possibility of utopia. But it does not have to be. It may equally well be an attack on certain tendencies in existing societies. Or it may be an exercise in pure imagination, passing no judgement on either utopia or the real world, but merely showing a partic-

* This is evident enough when one carefully reads the book and observes its tone. There is also external evidence. Some of Prof. Skinner's followers have started a movement to establish a school that will embody the principles outlined in *Walden Two*.

ular kind of nightmare embodied in a society of the author's creation. Sometimes the inverted utopia sets out to debunk the hope that evolutionary processes will inevitably lead to a nobler race of men and a better society. But the definition I have proposed will fit in any case.

The two brief definitions I have just given exclude a great deal of fantasy and whimsy, particularly in the spawning worlds of science fiction and children's stories. There one often finds other societies that are very different from anything in the newpapers or history books, but no attempt is made to present them as either desirable or undesirable. They are different for the sake of being different, fantasy for fantasy's sake. It is hard to draw a sharp line. I suspect that the world of *Alice in Wonderland* is intended to say something, by both resemblance and contrast, about the 19th-century world of Lewis Carroll, just as *Gulliver's Travels* presupposes a familiarity with the England of the author's time. Neither of these books is footloose fantasy. For my purposes, I shall take Gulliver into account, and disregard Alice. The decision has a touch of the arbitrary in it. But I think it best to exclude most of the borderline cases and concentrate on books where there seems clear evidence the author is deliberately presenting a society, and a possible one, which he regards as either superior or inferior to the world he knows. Inasmuch as I have drawn the lines rather tightly, I shall leave undisturbed in their lurid covers most science fiction stories and fantasies, even though many of them have a strand of utopianism or dystopianism, and often merit attention for other reasons.

A further limitation I have imposed upon myself is to choose only books — utopian or dystopian — about a society that might *plausibly* come into being; the books must also, directly or indirectly, say something important about the human condition and man's possibilities. I can explain what I mean by mentioning some books I shall not treat. I have excluded utopias that are achieved through magical or supernatural means. One must never deny the possibility that the thing can happen, but mankind can hardly plan towards such a goal; therefore the books are useless for our purpose. I have also restricted myself to books that deal with the human race. I suppose I could have included C. S. Lewis's interplanetary trilogy, since his *hrossa*, *séroni* and *pfifltriggi* are rational beings and sufficiently like us to merit comparison, but it seemed best to make only marginal use of works that for my purposes are borderline. Still less useful to me are a great many science fiction novels about Bug-Eyed-Monsters or beings that are more like computing machines than men. Either is too alien to our condition. I further insist that evolution keep within bounds. W. O. Stapledon's *Last and First Men* is a magnificent prose epic of what evolution might do with two billion years: it shows us gigantic brains housed in ferro-concrete buildings, and the admirable 'eighteenth man', a species gifted with telepathy and a high-level group mind. But most of this is too far removed from our present psychic equipment to be very relevant.

Sometimes — particularly in the case of inverted utopias — an obviously true possibility is dramatised, but then there seems nothing much to say except that it is obviously true. *A Canticle for Leibowitz*, by Walter M. Miller, Jr., and Aldous Huxley's *Ape and Essence* both depict a very convincing return of the Dark Ages (or worse) after an atomic war. These two books make the same point as William Golding's *Lord of the Flies* — that civilisation is skin-deep. But most of us have always known that. In our explorations of paradise and hell we shall be looking for insights a little less obvious.

CHAPTER THREE

Man as Dreamer

WHY DO men dream utopian dreams?

Let me speculate. I think there are at least two reasons. The first is that man is an animal with imagination. He can conceive of things that do not yet exist, may never exist. This is the source of change and progress, in so far as progress is a reality. It is the capacity that makes possible the arts, new systems of government, the growth of science.

Put another way, man has the curious and awesome ability to transcend himself and nature. True, he is trapped in nature. He is a thing of molecules requiring daily food, and there is a built-in executioner in his body to guarantee that he will not live for ever. All the same, he is a strangely free prisoner of nature. He is not only alive; he knows he is alive. His imagination can roam the years before he was born and the years after he is no longer here.

Man, the strange animal, can seize on the faintest hints of possible realities and track them to their source. Experience of something that seems good leads him to conceive Goodness with a capital G; two crude diagrams give him a vision of perfect triangularity. In his daily life he has broken glimpses of love, justice, and beauty; these lead him to dream of a society in which these glimpses are a steady light, the daily reality. What I have just said is a commonplace. One can say many things about the human animal, but not that it is a contented vegetable. It is restless from birth, or at least a large percentage of its members are restless, always looking for new things, inventing new ideas, and trying them out.

My second speculation is plausible or not, depending upon one's theological presuppositions. If you do not share my theology, I think you can translate the speculation into your own vocabulary and it will still make sense. I believe man once lived in utopia, but does no longer, and that he is always trying to return. The name of his first utopia was Eden. I do not care whether one conceives of Eden as a tract of real estate or a purely metaphysical garden. It may never have existed 'in time'. But, however conceived, it is a part of our heritage. We want to go back. The flaming swords of angels bar the way. So we must create another garden, a new Eden.

We are haunted by memories of the original garden and that lost innocence. In our heart of hearts, we know that our race has not always lived in the world of historical time, a world shot through with oppression, misunderstanding, meaningless tragedy, cruelty, individual and collective insanity; a world only haphazardly redeemed by some moments and deeds of niggardly virtue and grudging magnanimity, and fugitive instants of compassion and love. It was not always so. Metaphysically if not historically, it was not always so. The poor thing we commonly call our 'human nature' was not our first nature; it is a pathological condition.

We cannot reconcile ourselves to 'making the best of things', for such a reconciliation is an affirmation that our exile is permanent. We are Displaced Persons, but our old homeland burns and glows in our hearts. If we cannot literally return to it, we can build as close a facsimile as possible. Augustine and his City of God, Calvin at Geneva, the founding fathers in America planting their white churches in the green Canaan of the wilderness, Thomas Jefferson with his vision of the rational and benevolent society, the idealists of the French and Russian revolutions, the countless small bands of men and women in the 19th century who established co-operative communities to make Eden come true — all these were D.P.'s trying to create a new Eden in place of the old. And where there is no immediate opportunity to build Eden, men dream dreams and write books.

The folklore of the world bears eloquent testimony to man's knowledge that he is a D.P. Golden ages of the past or of the future, blessed isles barely out of sailing reach, and in modern science fiction the paradises in remote galaxies all record our wistful but unshakeable conviction that we are living in an alien land, amid alien corn that is bitter to the tongue.

The 'paradise regained' of folklore may be short on the theological virtues and spiritual elevation, but it still testifies to our nagging discontent. Neither Plato nor Augustine nor More would be content in the Eden of the Big Rock Candy Mountains, but in the words of the hobo ballad there is a picture of utopia as many humble men conceive it:

> In the Big Rock Candy Mountains
> You never change your socks,
> And little streams of alcohol
> Come a-trickling down the rocks.
> The box cars are all empty,
> And the railroad bulls are blind.
> There's a lake of stew and whisky, too,
> You can paddle all round 'em in a big canoe
> In the Big Rock Candy Mountains.
>
> O — the buzzing of the bees in the cigarette trees
> Round the soda-fountain,
> Where the lemonade springs and the bluebird sings
> In the Big Rock Candy Mountains.

There's a land that's fair and bright,
In the Big Rock Candy Mountains
Where handouts grow on bushes,
And you sleep out every night.
Where the box cars are all empty
And the sun shines every day.
O I'm bound to go, where there ain't no snow,
Where the rain don't fall and the wind don't blow,
In the Big Rock Candy Mountains.*

As a matter of fact, this vision of utopia is not completely alien to the dreams of the great utopians. The economy of abundance and the radical re-ordering of human relationships are familiar goals. The emphasis on the physical and friendly beauty of the landscape recalls the humanised natural world of H. G. Wells's utopias and many others. Thus the lowliest utopian vision has points in common with the loftiest attempts to imagine a new Eden.

My concern, however, is neither with folklore nor with the actual utopian communities that idealists of wildly varied sorts have tried to establish, but with books. The honour of being the first literary utopian must be disputed between Plato and the Hebrew prophets. Plato is usually accorded the honour, and certainly his blueprints are the more detailed; in particular, he pays greater attention to the practical necessities of government and social organisation. But if the prophets are short on technical blueprints, they are long on intensity of vision.

Fom one point of view, the prophets were not forward-looking utopians at all. They came to the fore after the Hebrews had abandoned their old migratory ways and settled down on farms and in cities. It was as though Bedouin Arabs or American Indians were suddenly plunged into a

* From *Folk Song: U.S.A.*, Lomax, N.Y., Duell, Sloane & Pierce.

much more complicated network of relationships. The money-lender reared his ugly head; the rich grew richer and bought up the holdings of the poor, or foreclosed on them. Class distinctions that had been minor in the desert became major, and galling. To the prophets, it often seemed that the way out was back to the pristine virtues of the desert, when — as legend at least would have it — men had walked humbly with God and dealt justly and mercifully with one another. Probably the prophets rarely thought of themselves as proposing a new vision; they were summoning men back to an old one. Since their idea of the past was as much legend as fact — and since the old simplicities were impossible in the new network of social and economic relationships — the prophets tend to be too simple in their analysis of what is wrong, and too simple in their remedies. They are sociologically naïve.

But that is only one half of the picture, and the less important half. An idealised image of the past may have helped inspire the prophets, but something else, perhaps God, helped more. The essence of what they said was not just a back-to-the-simple-life message. They were the custodians of a continuing and developing vision of what human existence might be anywhere, any time, and among all men. Their romantic backward glance was little more than a way of focusing upon the timeless vision that grew before their eyes.

Each prophet* has his particular flavour. Amos, in the 8th century B.C., is the earliest of the literary prophets, and thus has some claim to being the pioneer utopian. Like most of the prophets, he was poorly adjusted to the spirit of the times. Jeroboam II was still reigning as king of Israel; peace and prosperity prevailed. The kingdom had been extended until

* For a brief and interesting discussion of the prophets as utopians, see *The History of Utopian Thought*, Chapter II, by Joyce Oramel Hertzler.

it rivalled that of the by now almost mythical David. The standard of living was good and rising — horses, chariots, stone houses, ivory palaces. God was not being neglected either. In the midst of the revels at the autumn festival, celebrated at Bethel in 760 B.C., an impressive number of sacrifices was offered. The festival was abruptly interrupted by Amos, a sycamore dresser and herdsman, who announced the imminent decay and destruction of all the luxury and splendour. What he saw about him was, in his eyes, rotten to the root. It was based on the exploitation of man by man, and a false worship that put empty ritual in the place of justice. He issued the call, the familiar one — Repent and reform before it is too late: 'Seek the Lord and ye shall live' (Amos 5: v. 6). 'Seek good and not evil.' (v. 14). Of ritual when the spirit is lacking, he warned, in God's name: 'Though ye offer me burnt offerings and your meat offerings, I will not accept them: neither will I regard the peace offerings of your fat beasts.' (v. 22).

Amos discerned a law of cause and effect operating in history. A corrupt and unjust nation would be destroyed by a stronger power, in this case the Assyrians. God would *use* the Assyrians. But what of Amos's positive message? He offers no detailed solutions. He does not propose a constitutional convention, a new system of land tenure, or the abolition of the class system. From the viewpoint of modern sociology, he is guilty of 'pseudo-transformationism'. He believed that if men truly repented and turned to God and resolved to practise justice among their neighbours, all evils would be cured. He had no awareness that structural changes might have to be made in society itself before the pure life and the practice of justice could become a live option. It was as though the American founding fathers had shouted at every street corner, 'Life, liberty, and the pursuit

34

of happiness', but had never held a constitutional convention.

He was naïve, but his vision lives on when the practical plans of shrewder men are forgotten. Despite their wide differences in tone and emphasis, the same naïveté is characteristic of Hosea, Isaiah, Jeremiah, Ezekiel and Deutero-Isaiah. A partial exception is the theocratic Ezekiel who conceives of the purified nation as a worshipping community, and draws up the most specific plans for the proper maintenance of ritual holiness in worship and life. But even he is vague about the practical, everyday details of ordinary life. None of the prophets ever gets down very much to the matters that a modern economist or sociologist would put first on his list. From beginning to end there is the assumption that, if all is right between man and God and man and man, the imbalances and injustices of society will right themselves. To believe this is like saying that if everyone had gone to church every Sunday in the 1920's, the Great Depression would never have occurred.

The prophets are utopian in spirit, and their teachings have nourished the utopian hope through the ages. But they are not 'practical' utopians. They would never have been employed by Plato as guardians or by H. G. Wells as samurai. Though their influence on mankind is greater and more enduring than that of the practical utopians, they are marginal to our present purposes, and I shall say no more about them. Nor shall I discuss the apocalyptic writings that flourished shortly before and after the time of Christ. These are still more other-worldly, depending heavily on God's catastrophic intervention to change the human condition.

For partly similar and partly dissimilar reasons, I am omitting Christ and his teachings. One could certainly argue that his Kingdom of God is a utopia and a model one — a restoration of Eden that is more than restoration. But to fit him into the same historical pattern with Plato, More, Bellamy, and Wells involves too many violent adjustments. Many utopian experiments and theories have flowed directly from his teachings, ranging from the monastic movements to Augustine's ambiguous City of God (was it on earth or in heaven or both?) and the many actual utopian communities established by religious groups. Mainly, however, from my specialized viewpoint, the importance of Christ is that he fed the stream of utopian dreaming and thinking, and offered a set of ideals that challenged the utopian planners.

It appears that we shall have to back-track to Plato. He is the first full-fledged utopian. He offers not merely a vision but the accompanying blueprints.

CHAPTER FOUR

Plato and Company

PLATO, LIKE the Hebrew prophets, lived at a particular place and time. The place was Athens, when its sun had passed a little beyond noon. Grim Sparta, whose customs and laws were later described with such admiration by Plutarch, was proving more than the military equal of the Athens that once had led a victorious coalition against the Persian Empire.

To Plato it seemed that the time had come to buckle up tighter. Athens was too anarchistic, too individualistic, too much set on luxury and self-indulgence. It needed discipline and the sterner virtues. It needed, in fact, an infusion of Spartan strength. Plato's *The Republic* is in part an effort to show how the best features of Athens and Sparta could be combined.

The Republic is so well known to literate readers that I shall mention only a few of its points. First of all, it is interesting but not surprising that Plato made his utopia a small city-state. He could hardly have done otherwise. Athens and Sparta were his immediate models. If a Republic was to be a republic, it had to be small enough for the citizens to assemble and literally make their voices heard. It remained for the utopians of more than two thousand years later, with improved communications and transport, to dream of a utopia coterminous with the globe.

Like many of his utopian successors, Plato had only moderate faith in the judgement and versatility of the average person. He believed in specialisation, with strong but

37

benevolent direction from the top. His society is divided into three classes, each of which embodies a particular virtue. The ruling class consists of philosophers, who have arrived at their position by a long education leading to the direct perception of the metaphysical Good. Their virtue is, of course, wisdom.

The second class is the guardian — soldiers, public officials, and the like. They have been educated to the point where they can practise their special virtue, courage, but they have not made the final ascent to pure wisdom. These two upper classes seem not wholly distinct; there is some overlapping of function.

The great mass of the people are the workers — artisans, tradesmen, etc. — and the inevitable slaves. Little is said about them. They are taken for granted. Their virtue is temperance, which means self-restraint and obedience.

Finally, the virtue that holds the classes together and cements the state is justice. When every man is doing his proper job, he is exercising justice and the state is just.

To make sure that individuals merge their own desires with the welfare of the state, Plato strikes at two bulwarks of individualism: property and the family. It is not altogether clear whether his prohibitions apply to everyone — probably he is thinking of the two upper classes, which alone have any authority. Private property is abolished. A system of communism is established, not to satisfy the clamours of the envious, but to remove a prime source of selfishness. The family is also done away with, or extended — it is a question of semantics. At any rate, begetting and child-bearing become the province of the state, which exercises strong eugenic controls.

Baldly summarised, Plato's Republic sounds like permanent mobilisation or a concentration camp, but to him it was the reconciliation of the individual and his society.

38

Plato and Company

Political and moral imperatives are merged; man is completely the political animal. His absorption into the state is further ensured by a system of education as much moral and metaphysical as factual and physical; by state supervision of rank and occupation; and by censorship of the arts to make sure that they encourage the right attitudes. Effeminate music is banned, and the scandalous Homer is prohibited.

Education is indeed the key to the whole system. The finest (but rarest) product of education is a true philosopher. It is assumed that the state will be well and justly run by the philosophers, for they have beheld the metaphysical Good with unclouded eyes, and can dispassionately work at making it prevail in all the affairs of civic life.

Plato will haunt us as we swiftly move through the centuries towards our own. For instance, his philosopher-rulers are a stock in trade of subsequent imaginary societies. In H. G. Wells's *A Modern Utopia* we meet them almost unchanged — the samurai. They reappear in a coarsened form as the inner circle of the Party in Orwell's *Nineteen Eighty-Four*. Plato's second class also has many descendents. The cringing outer-circle Party members of Orwell's book are the dwindled inheritors. Most obviously of all, the third class — the metaphysically unwashed — corresponded to the slaves and criminals of More's *Utopia* as well as to the animal-like but carefree proles of *Nineteen Eighty-Four*.

The eugenic control of mating and the state's role in child-rearing are a theme running through many utopias and anti-utopias, ranging from a mild form in More's *Utopia* (the betrothed have a chance to see each other naked before marriage, to make sure there are no blemishes) to the *Brave New World*'s hatcheries. It is important to remember that Plato's opposition to the traditional family was not based on the longing for a private harem. He wished to deprive the ruling classes of monogamous marriage so that private passions and interests would not sway them. His attitude towards sex and women is crisp and business-like. He releases women from the kitchen and bedroom and gives them such perfect equality that they too can carry a spear or become philosopher-rulers.

It is almost true — but not quite — that subsequent utopias can be defined as 'Plato plus footnotes', and that the dystopias are 'Plato turned sour'. Plato supplies the great archetype. He shows how the happiness of the individual and that of the state can be completely merged; the individual clothes himself in the state and is good for ever. Other utopias will make less sweeping claims and demands; some of the dystopias will demand more. But Plato is the benchmark from which all observations and commentaries must start and to which reference must constantly be made.

After Plato, the utopian dream lies dormant for two thousand years. Not quite, of course. Plutarch writes of an idealised Sparta. The Kingdom of God haunts men as an impossible possibility. Augustine sketches the City of God, and men wonder whether it is another name for the Church. The supreme utopia, Heaven, gleams, but beyond the curtain of death. Legends, as always, circulate about golden ages, blessed isles of the west, lands of Cockaigne. Meanwhile, men set themselves to creating brick-and-stone, flesh-and-blood utopias: the monasteries, the medieval universities, Christian civilisation itself. But there is no major writer presenting in imaginary form a vision like that of the Republic.

It remained for a curious and appealing combination of scholar and dreamer, statesman and martyr, to write the next major utopia, and to invent the word. Thomas More, knight and later Saint, was an Erasmus-like figure. He knew his

Plato and Company

Plato, of course, and his Augustine, and his Gospels, and the influence of all three is evident in *Utopia* (1516).

If Plato wrote *The Republic* to reform Athens, More offered *Utopia* as a guide to the improvement of an England that badly needed it. He wished to show that poverty, crime, cruel punishments, invidious distinctions between classes are not in the order of nature, but are man's doing, and that man could equally well create a just and happy social order.

Utopia — which, as you will recall, means both 'no place' and 'good place' — is an island two hundred miles long and wide, with fifty-four large, well-planned cities, located so that each is no more than a day's walk from the next. Men work but six hours a day, which is sufficient to provide for the modest needs of all. The distinction between city man and rustic is eliminated by having everyone take a turn at farmwork — thus anticipating one of the proposals of *The Communist Manifesto*.

Government is carried on by officials elected directly or indirectly. Each thirty families selects a magistrate. A higher official rules over every ten magistrates. The magistrates, taken all together, constitute a kind of Senate which chooses the prince from a panel of four candidates presented by the people. The prince rules for life unless suspected of tyrannical ambitions. He is advised by a cabinet. The general picture is that of a benevolent monarchy with some rudimentary checks and balances, and a fair amount of popular control on the lower levels of government.

More is less concerned than Plato with metaphysical questions. His purpose is bluntly practical. None the less his actual proposals agree with many of Plato's. The attitude towards property is similar. More communises it to ensure a sufficient livelihood for all, and to eliminate the corrosive inequality between the rich and the poor. Since everyone has all the necessities of life, there is no need for robbery and theft. Money itself is abolished. The absurd adoration of gold is counteracted by the ingenuous device of making slave chains and chamber pots out of the metal. People dress in standardised and simple clothing. Utopia may not be a democracy, and there is no levelling of social distinctions, but at least it is a world in which there is little opportunity to flaunt one's status in the eyes of others. It also makes provision for free choice of occupation, and upward mobility.

Again like Plato, More attaches great importance to education. It is life-long, and includes elevated conversations and lectures at the communal meals, as well as formal instruction. The purposes are moral and practical. The end product is somehow characteristically English — persons who may not contemplate the metaphysical Good but who are equipped with common sense and decent attitudes towards their fellows.

More's greatest quarrel with Plato is over the family, which the Athenian concedes only to the lower orders. The Englishman was after all a Christian, living at a time when families were still patriarchal and often included a number of generations and offshoots under one roof. He continues the familiar system. The state is the supervisor of marriages, but its hand is light. An Englishman of the 16th century on a visit to Utopia would note with approval that wives obey their husbands, children their parents, and the younger children serve the older ones, a hierarchal arrangement that would have met with Confucius' benign commendation as well as the Church's. The oldest father in the household is the final authority until he passes into dotage; the power then goes to the next oldest father.

The principal safeguards against too family-centred an existence are the communal halls where most choose to dine, and the widespread practice of adoption when one family has many children and another has few or none.

More was not describing a Christian commonwealth but the kind of society that men, by light of natural reason, could create. It is probably for this reason that he treats religion as he does. The result is strikingly modern. One thinks of the college campuses where a diluted and inoffensive religious service is held for the entire student body and faculty, with the understanding that those who attend it will supplement it, if they wish, by going also to particular churches that more definitely embody their private beliefs. In Utopia, the people assemble in a great interdenominational temple for the generalised worship of the God revealed to natural reason. They can belong to more specialised cults and attend their workshop as much as they wish. Proselytising, if gently done, is permitted. The generalised if vague deism of the official religion is a social bond between the overwhelming majority of the people, and does no violence to any man's conscience. Even atheists are permitted to exist, though they cannot serve in the administration. There is never any attempt to convert them by force.

Utopia is less primed for war than the Republic. True, Utopia is not above a bit of conquest for additional *Lebensraum,* but its citizens prefer as far as possible, by wile and guile, to keep their hands unbloody. They are skilled at psychological and fifth-column techniques, and if events come to the blood-letting stage, the brunt of battle is borne mainly by foreign mercenaries.

I suppose by now I have revealed my bias. Though I am not buying a one-way ticket to either Plato's Republic or More's Utopia, if I had to make a choice it would be for the latter. More is less dourly schematic. He pays more respect to long-established human inclinations, such as having a wife who is all your own. He is less doctrinaire. He does not

43

subordinate life in all its crazy but wonderful luxuriance and variety to the cold demands of a dubious metaphysic. You could accustom yourself to Utopia. I should rather like to spend a long vacation there, listening to the edifying conversations of the grave elders. It would also be pleasant to live in a country that can persuade other peoples to fight their wars for them.

Not half bad. It is only gradually that another feeling insinuates itself. It is more an intuition than a reasoned objection. For Utopia, though not as schematic as the Republic, still smells too strongly of the drafting board, the compass and dividers. These fifty-four cities, so carefully planned, so identical, as indistinguishable as the newer crop of American suburbs. The neat precision of the integration of country and town. The public character of private life. The ever-present sense of the watchful eye, alert to prevent any excessive upthrust of individualism and eccentricity. It begins to seem like a paradise for men in grey flannel suits.

One wonders how a Thoreau or Plato's master, Socrates, would fare in Utopia. Every time Thoreau went to Boston he would have to secure a travel permit and go in a group. Would he be left alone at Walden? Still more, what of Shakespeare? There's the test. If a Utopia is not capacious enough for Socrates to ask embarrassing questions of the Prince, for Thoreau to waste his time at Walden, and for Shakespeare to conceive a *Hamlet*, write it, produce it — it is not the land of man's deepest desires. It may be in nine ways out of ten better than any society existing at a given moment in time; it may be the best that reasonable men can hope and plan for; it is still not the haunting vision.

And soon, too, the inescapable question will not lie quiet. If the prince and his advisers are to be the controllers and all-seeing eyes of Utopia, who is to watch and control them? Who is to guard the guardians? The safeguards seem flimsy. Perhaps it is peculiarly because of the period in which we live, but we find it difficult to imagine men wise enough and good enough to exercise power on the higher levels of the Utopian pyramid. The man who wields power may not line his pockets or stock his palace with the fairest daughters of the land, but he is constantly tempted to play at being God and to use those beneath him as raw materials to mould into shapes satisfying to his ego. We should like more checks and balances.

Yet, no sooner do one's nerves begin to twitch apprehensively at the corruptions and abuses that might turn Utopia into dystopia, than another voice seems to ask: 'What are you looking for? See the world you live in. Is it free of corruption and the abuse of power? If Utopia has an equal share of corruption and misuse of power, wouldn't it still be better than what you've got? At least it would have started out good, whereas your world is one that has been ailing from the first moment. Better a sound body that catches measles, than a body with rickets from birth — and then measles.'

I must leave More's Utopia at this point, with suspended judgement and honestly ambivalent emotions. More opened wide the floodgates of utopian thinking, but at first the waters were in no hurry to flow. It was more than a century before the publication of another unmistakably major work, Johann Valentin Andreae's *Christianopolis* (1619). A humanist and Lutheran, Andreae aims at depicting an ideal Christian city. It has a warm, human quality about it. The basic social unit is the guild, so that men's social life revolves spontaneously around their work. The guilds are largely self-governing, a kind of grassroots democracy. Science is studied as a means of improving technology. Education is for all. Everyone works, using materials from the common storehouse. There is free scope for individual inventiveness and fancy. Public morale is such that everyone is prepared to undertake any task, however irksome, that the general good requires.

The family system is more modern than in *Utopia*. The typical family consists simply of the husband, wife and their children. Mothers care for their children up to the age of six, when the community and its school system take over, though parents can always visit their children as often as they wish. The school is run as a miniature republic, and the teaching methods have rather a flavour of American-style Progressive Education. Great use is made of visual aids, such as mural paintings to illustrate natural history. The teachers are the cream of humanity, not 'men from the dregs of human society nor such as are useless for other occupations'.

Christianopolis, infused with a glowing and gentle religion, and happily at work with abounding opportunity for self-expression, is a more jolly place than either the Republic or Utopia. It is assuredly a more attractive home than Bacon's *The New Atlantis*, described in a fragment of that name published in 1627. Bacon's city is a mosaic of Plato and More. There is equality of sexes *à la* Plato, and young folk serving their elders *à la* More. But sober simplicity is missing. Bacon revels in descriptions of satins, velvets, jewels and ceremonial garb, so that his city sounds like the French court just before the guillotine descended.

The New Atlantis contains one shape of things to come. That is Salomon's house, a research institute. Here one discerns the faint, ghostly outlines of the great research foundations of our times. Bacon may describe the activities of the House in infantile language, and make it seem as much a magician's studio as a laboratory — after all, science

46

and magic had not quite decided on a divorce in the early 17th century — but he at least sensed the way the real world, and most provinces of the utopian world, would be moving.

Thomas Campanella's *City of the Sun* was written about the same time as *The New Atlantis*. An Italian, and Dominican friar, Campanella was continually under suspicion for unorthodox views, both those he actually entertained and some that he did not. He was put to the question by the Spanish Inquisition seven times, and spent twenty-seven years in prison, where he wrote his book. Finally released, he journeyed to Rome. Pope Urban VIII tried to protect him, but eventually he had to flee, dressed as a servant of the French ambassador. Richelieu befriended him in Paris and he received a royal pension. The persecutions were at last over. He lived to the age of seventy-one in the Convent of the Dominicans.

The City of the Sun shows, as one would expect, the influence of both More and Plato — the latter in particular — plus some intriguing features of its own. The inhabitants are reasonably orthodox Christians, though astrology seems more functional in their lives than the Gospels. The conjunction of the stars determines the planting of trees and the mating of men and women. The principal ruler is a kind of high priest, Hoh or Metaphysicus, elected from among the better educated. He is assisted by three princes of equal rank, also elected: Power, Wisdom and Love. The four work together, but Hoh always has the last word. Crime has been abolished by eliminating the needs and selfish desires that motivate it. The economic system is communistic. Matings are arranged by the state. Those persons who happen to fall in love on their own are permitted to exchange amorous verses and garlands, but that is all, unless the state grants its eugenic approval. The couples chosen for

47

breeding do not ordinarily feel love but rational friendship towards each other, rather like the houyhnhnm in *Gulliver's Travels*. As if all this were not communal enough, the other-directed way of life is reinforced by the familiar public dining-halls and by dormitory life.

Everyone labours, and there is no need of slaves. The hardest or most disagreeable work carries special esteem. Women have their equality. Sanitation and medicine are highly developed. Most people live to a flourishing hundred years; some make it to two hundred.

The City of the Sun is a quaint hodgepodge of Christianity, astrology, and metaphysics-on-the-planning-board, and it shows exceedingly little grasp of the psychological needs that militate against so schematic a utopia. But it stands in the direct line of utopian development, particularly in the emphasis on eugenics, education, and the aristocracy of merit and education. All of these features, gleaming brightly or perverted into lurid nightmares, will face us again and again in other books.

The 17th century was rich in utopias, but the ones already discussed will serve as types. One other might be mentioned briefly, *Oceana*, by James Harrington. Written in the time of Cromwell, it was more a proposal for a new political constitution than a complete utopia in the grand manner. It advocates such now familiar ideas as the importance of written laws, wide distribution of property, the secret ballot, indirect election, rotation of offices, and a bicameral legislature. A feeling for 'checks and balances' and the realities of political life infuses this highly practical utopia, which Harrington wrote in the hope that Cromwell might implement it. Meanwhile Charles II was biding his time, and with his return the utopian prospects darkened.

The 18th century is full of imaginary voyages and geographical fantasies, but is poor in full-scale utopias. Perhaps the energies of men were directed more towards real-life planning, as the American and still more the French revolution made possible some extensive attempts to reorder society. I shall therefore let the century slide by, and move on to the 19th century, which shares with the 17th the distinction of being the richest in utopian literature.

Of the 19th century utopias, the most important is Edward Bellamy's *Looking Backward* (1888). The work of an American, it is a winsome and winning book, aglow with gentle love of humanity. Its narrative framework is 'the sleeper awakes'. Julian West, an upper-class Bostonian, goes into a state of suspended animation in 1887, and awakes in A.D. 2000 to find a much improved Boston. There is a decorous love story, involving a romance with a girl descended from his old sweetheart, but the main point is what has happened to Boston, America and the whole world.

The old Boston, as described in *Looking Backward*, was dirty, noisy, exploitative, divided by savage and unjust schisms of education, money and class. The rich had been getting richer, the poor no richer. Big business was becoming monopolistic; the middle-sized fellow was being squeezed out. When West awakes he finds that the evolutionary process has gone to its logical culmination. The nation has peacefully taken over the means of production; it has become the universal trust. The great enterprises are rationally directed to the general good. Systematic planning is possible for the first time. Boston itself is much cleaned up; crime is reduced; marriages are for love instead of money or prestige. Human nature, whatever one means by this slippery term, has not changed, but human circumstances have and the new environment brings out the most generous and altruistic impulses.

In a sense, a benevolent sense, the new America is now a

garrison state. Everyone is conscripted for twenty-four years of labour, from the age of twenty-one to forty-five. Generally, a person can work at tasks most suitable to his talents and inclinations. Particularly hard jobs are rewarded by shorter hours. A semi-military discipline prevails during the apprenticeship period. For anyone unwilling to work, there is the persuasion of solitary confinement on bread and water, an item that stands out starkly in a singularly gentle book. Money has been abolished; government-issued credit-cards take its place. The state has withered away; or rather, it has merged with the economic administration. Now that exploitative competition is ended — throughout the world, all of which has gone socialistic — war is no more. International trade is conducted by a supranational council, with a simple system of book-keeping.

So far, Bellamy's scheme sounds like reasonably orthodox Socialism. He refuses, however, to follow the more extreme strand of Socialist thought in its campaign against private life. His family system is firmly Victorian, except, as I have already mentioned, marriage is now for pure motives of love. A flexible compromise between family privacy and public convenience is achieved. For instance, laundry is done at public establishments, very low priced. Meals are publicly cooked, but each family can have a private dining-room in the great public restaurants and order the particular meals they desire.

Science and technology are developing on schedule, and the reader is offered such conveniences as music and sermons via telephone. We are told that literature and the arts are flourishing as never before, but unfortunately no specimens are included.

Women are equal; the occasional criminals are treated, not punished; education is universal. All in all, though that solitary cell and its dry bread wait always in the background, it is a much more humane world than the Boston of the 1880's, and Julian West is well advised to stay awake this time and marry the descendent of his old sweetheart.

Bellamy wrote a book and started a movement. Bellamy societies proliferated in Europe and America, provoking an ideological and literary counter-attack — but that must be discussed later. The honour of inspiring concrete political consequences belongs also to Theodor Hertzka, a distinguished Viennese economist, whose *Freeland — A Social Anticipation* was published two years after Bellamy's book. In Austria and Germany alone, nearly a thousand local societies sprang up to put his principles into action. Sixteen pioneers finally headed for Uganda to found a colony, but a combination of nature's inhospitality and British suspicions frustrated the eager utopians, and the project petered out.

The British suspected socialist designs. In actual fact, Hertzka was an economist of the Manchester school. His aim was not to destroy capitalism but to make it work, mainly through spreading the ownership of property as widely as possible and setting up a series of co-operatives or joint stock companies by people in similar lines of work. His proposals were based not on altruism but on the individual's enlightened self-interest.

Hertzka devoted his main attention to economics, being as convinced as any Marxist that most other problems will solve themselves if the economic foundation of society is right. He is forward-looking and modern in the details of his utopia: he welcomes machinery and anticipates automobiles and motorised gondolas; he foreshadows the welfare state with his provisions for the adequate maintenance of children, the aged and the incapacitated. In a general way, his book points towards the modified capitalism prevailing today in western Europe and the United States. This utopia offers no stylised sages in tunics and sandals; it propounds no metaphysical absolutes on which society must be based; it is a brisk and practical proposal, made by a man who had small patience with most utopian daydreaming.

Our hop-skip-and-jump tour of utopia may now come to an end with a book that in many ways sums up and climaxes the classical utopian tradition. Appropriately enough, it was published soon after the turn of the century, when the glow of 19th-century optimism was still bright, and before the brighter glow of massed artillery in Flanders engulfed it. The author was H. G. Wells, a man far more complex than either his admirers or detractors have usually recognised. There was a deep streak of pessimism in him, which found expression in such dystopian tales as *The Time Machine* and *A Story of the Days to Come*. But he had his optimistic periods, times when it seemed that mankind was showing some hopeful signs of rationality and altruism and that the human venture could be guided in good directions. It was during one of these times of hope that he wrote *A Modern Utopia*.

This is no flight of fancy, no voyage into whimsy. It is a sober attempt to imagine what kind of society men would create if they really used their heads and worked at it. The result is one of the most plausible utopias ever written. It recognises certain persistent facts: there will always be failures, antisocial people, outright criminals. Special provision is made for these. Failures can turn to a kind of public works programme and earn a passable though not luxurious living. As for criminals, first offenders and any offenders under twenty-five are sent to special disciplinary schools in faraway areas. Those who are incorrigible, together with drunkards, drug addicts and the like, are exiled to remote islands where they are left to carry on their own way of life, with guards to keep them from escaping. The insane receive the best possible care and treatment.

In this utopia there is a cross between socialism and old-fashioned individualism. The World State — for this utopia covers the planet — owns all the land and sources of food and energy. Directly or through its subdivisions it leases out these resources. The government and its regional authorities are also responsible for public order, roads, eugenic matters, research, etc. The individual may own those things 'that become, as it were, by possession, extensions and expressions of his personality' — clothing, tools, jewels, books, art objects that he has created or bought, and other items of the sort. He can even bequeath such possessions, subject only to a small inheritance tax. If he acquires a house and furniture, the tax is slightly higher. Any other property is so heavily taxed at death that most of it passes to the state, though special exemptions are provided if the property is earmarked for the education of his children.

Wells's utopia, with its superb means of transportation, is one in which people are constantly on the go — looking for work in other parts of the world, taking vacations, indulging in simple tourism. Constant travel and migration have developed a one-world psychology; the old national parochialisms have faded out.

No war is waged against the machine. It is employed to eliminate dreary or degrading work and to make possible a high level of productivity and a fair portion of leisure time for all.

The state takes a lively interest in human reproduction, to prevent over-population or a deterioration in genetic quality. Two persons seeking marriage must satisfy the state that they are solvent, physically adequate and free of transmissible disease. There is a waiting period after application before final consent is given. The customs and laws encourage the permanence of marriage, at least until the last child no longer needs the mother, but provision is made for divorce in real cases of incompatibility. Children born outside of marriage are cared for by the state; the parent who offends a second time is sterilised.

The feature of Wells's utopia that links it most closely with Plato is the ruling class, the samurai. They are an order of men and women who have dedicated themselves to a more demanding and austere way of life than the common man is expected to follow. Any reasonably competent adult who has reached the age of twenty-five may enlist, though a college background is desirable. The samurai overcome self-indulgence by renouncing tobacco, alcohol and narcotics. They may not act, sing, or perform personal services, except medicine and surgery, nor may they have servants. There is no vow of celibacy, but a samurai marries only another samurai, or at least a woman who accepts the Woman's Rule, a modified discipline that puts her routine in harmony with her husband's.

The samurai, forbidden the luxury of cigarettes, are also denied the thrills of 'dramatically lit altars, organ music, and incense', but are encouraged to be religious in more severe ways. For at least one week each year a samurai must go into some solitary place, away from all other human beings, and devote himself to the rugged life and meditation.

Trained and toughened in body, mind and spirit by a discipline half military, half monastic, the samurai are the administrators of the country; indeed, practically all political power is in their hands. Their numbers are gradually increasing. It is hoped that in time most of the population will belong.

. . . . .

Plato and Company

Our brief tour of assorted utopias is now at an end.* It has by-passed one whole tributary to the utopian stream — the 'Arcadian utopia' or the 'utopia of escape', as Lewis Mumford calls it — such delightful books as James Hilton's *Lost Horizon* and Austin Tappan Wright's *Islandia*. We have kept strictly to the mainstream — utopias that imply not a snug retreat from the bustling world but conscious *planning* to reshape that world.

At least the sampling has been sufficient to indicate the variety of utopianism. We found, for instance, that utopia cannot be labelled either 'left' or 'right'. Very often it has a socialist or communist bias, but it can also be dedicated to capitalistic values, as witness *Freeland*.

When you look at the long sweep of utopian writing from Plato to Wells, it is easy to see the directions in which utopia has evolved. It has simply kept pace with the evolving consciousness and attitudes of Western man. For example, the role of religion has, with some exceptions, declined. At least, religion of any traditional sort plays a diminishing role as the 19th century is reached. There may still be a strong religious quality to the way of life, but it is likely to be more a matter of powerfully felt ethical obligations, or devotion to society and the human race.

A second change, more sharply evident, is that Darwin has taken up his home in utopia. His influence has led more imaginative writers to dream of mental telepathy or other new psychic equipment. Stapledon, in *Last and First Men*, speculates on the possibilities of both guided and unguided evolution, and shows one human species with a third eye on top of the head for gazing at the heavens. These biological speculations are of little immediate concern to a race still remarkably standardised in its physical heritage, but the idea

* The reader who wishes to explore more of them will find useful bibliographies in many of the books listed in the Appendix.

of evolution, as applied to social and political institutions, is more plausible. It is one of the main reasons that 19th- and 20th-century utopias tend to be less static than their predecessors. Wells and many modern utopians conceive of utopia not as a final perfection but as a goal and movement towards a goal; it is a *process*. In their terms, to be utopian is simply to have a utopian sense of direction, and work at it.

A third characteristic of the 19th- and 20th-century utopias is that they usually take economics seriously. More would have been aghast if anyone had told him that methods of production and distribution *determine* the psychological, cultural and spiritual life of the people. The modern utopias, when they give primacy to economics, may stem either from Marx or Manchester or some private revelation, but they make the point that economic processes must be rightly ordered if you want good human relations and a flourishing culture. In the technical, philosophic sense of the word, they are less 'idealistic' than their predecessors. They suspect that ideas do not come from the metaphysical blue, but are by-products of the bread-and-butter life of man.

In the fourth place, the trinity of science, technology and machinery becomes more evident in utopia. Here again, as always, I am disregarding the Arcadian utopias, which are likely to suppress the machine before it gets a headstart, or indulge in machine-smashing. The educational system of modern utopias usually includes more units in science than in Latin; Solomon's house is expanded; science is put to work doing all its benevolent tasks, such as lengthening the life span, curing diseases, increasing the productivity of land, providing the technology that will lead to labour-saving machinery. If slavery is rare in the modern utopia, it is partly because machines abound.

Such are some of the newer trends in utopia. But the

strands of continuity are equally striking. The keyword from Plato to Wells is *planning*. Utopia is the dream of replacing societies that have grown haphazardly by a society that knows what the good life is and draws up definite plans for bringing it into existence.

CHAPTER FIVE

The Composite Utopia

I AM tempted to write yet another utopian novel, one that would combine the most common features of the main-stream-utopias. But the thing is impossible. Anyone who has prowled even casually in this literary and subliterary thicket knows that the variety is too great. Every generalisation must be hedged about with half a page of footnotes. None the less, you might find it interesting to hear one man's general impression of utopia, as the vision has existed from Plato to the present moment. I shall omit the footnotes.*

To begin with, I have several times hinted that utopia is likely to be more humanistic than theocentric. Utopia does not depend on miracles and divine intervention. It counts on man to do his own work. This doesn't mean that utopia has to be godless. Occasionally its religion is some recognisable form of Christianity. It may be just barely recognisable, as in Edgar Mittelhölzer's *Shadows Move Among Them*, a delightful story of a jungle utopia (of sorts) led by a very liberal Christian minister who tells ghost stories in lieu of sermons, and celebrates the Holy Communion with soda pop and buns. More commonly, the religion is a vague deism, plus golden rule ethics. At times it shades off into a worshipful sense of obligation towards the community, the human race, or the evolutionary process. Some-

---

* Except for this one — to say that my treatment of the subject in this chapter has been greatly influenced by the excellent analyses contained in *Touring Utopia: The Realm of Constructive Humanism*, by Frances Theresa Russell.

The Composite Utopia

times the physical universe is the object of adoration, as in Louis Sébastien Mercier's *Memoirs of the Year Two Thousand Five Hundred* (1772), published shortly before the French Revolution, in which 'first communion' consists of gazing through a telescope at the heavenly bodies and then peering through a microscope.*

Occasionally, though less often than one might expect, religion is completely lacking. More likely, when you take out naturalisation papers in utopia, you will be invited to participate in some mild religious services with no cutting edge, and you will be free to frequent more specialised cults, so long as they are not antisocial. But your main religious outlet will be your daily life — your dedication to utopia itself.

The moral standards of utopia also vary greatly from one book to another, but I have the general impression that utopia is not very bacchanalian. Life is real and earnest; one must do his appointed task. Too much individualistic self-expression, sexually or otherwise, may elicit frowns or worse. There is, however, adequate opportunity for socially-approved channels of self-expression, such as begetting and conceiving eugenic children, inventing useful processes, and composing odes to strengthen the social solidarity of the utopians.

In the more extreme utopias, one's duty to society becomes co-extensive with the whole of morality. Plato does not stand alone in this. I suppose if you are looking for real-life parallels you will think of the Communist standard of morality, which is that whatever aids the spread of Communism is moral, and whatever impedes it is immoral.

* See Glenn Negley and J. Max Patrick, *The Quest for Utopia: An Anthology of Imaginary Societies.* This book contains, sometimes in condensed form, a wide sampling of utopias, many of which are long out of print.

From Utopia to Nightmare

Like the Communists, the imaginary utopians are prone to think there can be no valid conflict between the happiness of the individual and that of his perfect society; morality and happiness both consist of being a good citizen.

As I look at the variety of family life in utopia, I am convinced that the composite utopian novel will never be written. You can find almost every pattern, including the complete abolition of the family; monogamy; polyandry; group marriage; and simply following the dictates of nature. But pick your utopia carefully. In the statistically average utopia, monogamy seems to win out. Often the permanence of marriage and marital fidelity are enforced by strict sanctions. But, though monogamy may win in the battle of comparative statistics, the family is likely to be somewhat devalued. It must fit into the social blueprint. Don't count on a lock for your front door; be prepared to eat in a communal dining hall. There is a good chance your children will be brought up in state nurseries, or at least that the state will assume total charge of their education, without the option of a private school. If you accumulate any property, the state may be your heir. Your wife, liberated from *Kinder*, *Küche*, and *Kirche*, is perhaps carrying a hoe beside you in the field, or a gun on the battlefront.

Another feature of utopia is that you may not find it too easy to get married in the first place. The state and its eugenic experts will look you over carefully and decide whether you will serve society by increasing its population. You may have to be more than eighteen, more than twenty-one; your occupational reliability can be investigated and the testers may work you over before you receive society's *nihil obstat*.

Anyone anxious to know how democracy fares will discover a variety of attitudes and arrangements in utopia, but for the most part utopia does not go the extreme of letting its citizens decide too much by popular vote. Sometimes utopia is managed by interlocking panels of experts, who rule by virtue of wisdom and general consent. Government as such may disappear. In his short story, *With the Night Mail* (1905) Rudyard Kipling depicts a world managed by the international Aerial Board of Control, which maintains enough order to make sure that air traffic is undisturbed; in effect the Board has eliminated government by becoming a government.

One common feature of utopia is a class of voluntary nobility or non-hereditary aristocracy, like Plato's philosophers and Wells's samurai. Where these exist, power rests with them. In those utopias that have democratic tendencies, there is often an elaborate system of pyramidical indirect elections, rather like the United States electoral college as it exists in theory. All in all, utopia seems more inclined to distrust the masses than the classes.

The ghost of Plato is vocal and all but visible in the social structure of utopia. His pattern — a three-class system — has remained virtually unchanged in many of his successors. The agonising problem of how to keep the rulers from becoming tyrants is usually disregarded or treated sketchily. If there are formal checks and balances, they are likely to be rudimentary. Reliance is usually placed on educating a disciplined and selfless class of rulers who will be free of private ambitions. From the utopian viewpoint, the United States constitution is a singularly hardbitten and cautious document, for it breathes the spirit of scepticism about human altruism and incorporates a complex system of checks, balances and restrictions, so that everybody is holding the reins on everybody else.

Education is nearly always a cornerstone of utopia. Sometimes, as in Plato, it is mostly or entirely for the upper levels, but usually it is for everyone. The sciences and

From Utopia to Nightmare

practical arts get more attention than the humanities, but there is sometimes a rigorous philosophic training, reinforced by practice in spiritual and psychological disciplines. Body and character building are stressed; so is social adjustment. In utopia, education is frequently inescapable. It pursues you at meal-times in the form of edifying discourses and conversations guided by grave elders; it invades your leisure in the guise of constructive and instructive recreational activities. But you need all of it you can get. Your future occupation and status may be directly dependent on how far and how well you progress in your education.

Many utopian novels simply mention the importance and availability of education, but do not offer curriculum plans. The opposite is true of work. Who does what is spelled out in detail. The chances are you will find yourself working for the highly centralised utopian government or one of its subdivisions, though if you choose the right utopia there may be adequate room for private enterprise. In any case, you will work. But you will not have to labour too hard. With everybody at work, and extravagance and conspicuous consumption curbed, the hours of labour can be as short as the most advanced trade unions now advocate. Your conditions of work will usually be pleasant. There may be a picnic-like merriment associated with the joys of work, as you and your companions sally forth to the daily job. The retirement age could be fifty or earlier.

Sometimes you are permitted to choose your occupation freely; but often various controls, direct or indirect, strongly influence your decision. Your degree of education may point you towards some vocations, or exclude you from others. You may be drafted, perhaps for a limited period of time, to do a certain kind of work. The wage scales can be manipulated in such a way that you will be encouraged to go into work where there is a shortage of labour.

The Composite Utopia

A fairly common feature of utopia is a kind of semi-military service for young people, to take care of the dirty work. It is their apprentice-stage towards full adult rights.

The economic system of utopia, as we have seen, varies almost as much as its family system, but socialism does seem more frequent than pure *laissez-faire*. Often there is a compromise, leaving large-scale operations to the state, but permitting the individual to be a craftsman or small farmer.

The favourite utopian art is architecture. Characteristically it is massive, functional, glistening and clean. Cities look as though they were laid out with straight-edge and T-square. The most magnificent works of architecture are not private homes but structures in the public sector: research centres, temples, transportation terminals, etc.

Of the other arts, music seems the most favoured. Plato recognised its value in welding society into a harmonious whole, and it continues to play this role. If you are not listening to lectures at meal-time you are probably enjoying background music of a socially desirable kind. Great civic occasions have special music. The remaining arts receive briefer attention. One gets the impression that in the composite utopia art does not exist for the sake of art; art is the handmaiden of society. This, of course, is Plato once more. The arts that serve some practical purpose or create desirable social attitudes are encouraged; the others are marginal, or, in some cases, are actively discouraged.

To the fashion designer, utopia is one of the lower circles of Hell. True, Bacon provides for gorgeous raiment, but most utopias stipulate something simple, easy to mass-produce. Often it is an unashamed uniform, practical and symbolic of social cohesion. The most favoured costume is some version of the Greek tunic and sandals. Elaborate ornaments and jewellery are usually suspect. In one or two

63

utopias, I might add, the uniform is the candour of nudity, but — whether for reasons of climate or aesthetics or as a survival of conventional morality — the nudist utopia is a rarity.

Most utopias like to keep an eye on you, for your own good and that of society. Statisticians and the supervisors follow you with a benevolent gaze. For travel within utopia you may need a kind of passport. More often, you simply report your change of address to the proper authorities. Sometimes there is a central bureau where elaborate data are kept on file in regard to each citizen. The entries on your card may determine whether you can borrow money, enter a certain profession, or get married. Wells, in *A Modern Utopia*, situates this master file in Paris, as an Englishman's tribute to the lucidity and order of the French mind. He pictures it as containing the individual's thumb-prints, his assigned number (which is also on his identity card), and full information on his occupational history, genetic characteristics, and marital status, as well as his criminal record if any. When you die your card is transferred to the inactive file, where you enjoy a classified immortality.

Even utopia must reckon with death, suffering and crime. Crime is reduced to a minimum by good social institutions. But when it does occur, it is treated with varying degrees of severity, ranging from death or slavery to loving care in a mental institution. Exile or ostracism is the most characteristic method of discipline. Often there is a distant island to which criminals and misfits are shipped. But crime is no great problem in utopia. A wholesome environment reduces it to small proportions and public opinion is more powerful than laws in most nations.

Suffering of the cruder sort is greatly reduced by a decent standard of living, the elimination of many diseases and general increase in health. The more subtle forms of suffering, like frustrated love and vague *Weltschmerz*, lend themselves less easily to direct cure, but the composite utopia assumes its way of life will offer such positive satisfactions that the old intensely personal griefs and agonies will be minor in comparison with the assured joys.

In utopia as everywhere else the attitude towards death is conditioned by the attitude towards life. For the typical utopian, life is intensely worth living as long as body and mind are functioning with reasonable efficiency. When they deteriorate too markedly, life ceases to appeal. The idea of euthanasia does not horrify the utopians. Even the devout More includes it, on a voluntary basis. In a number of utopias you will find a house of euthanasia (functional, clean, gleaming) where in surroundings suggestive of a resort hotel you can go in old age for a last fling and painless exit from utopia.

From eugenic birth to antiseptic extinction, utopia looks after you. The way I feel about utopia depends on the mood I am in. When life is too much with me, when newspaper headlines are appalling and my private affairs are in chaos, when everywhere I see humanity (which includes me) making a mess of things, then utopia glows. I am ready or almost ready to abandon my more bizarre quirks and private dreams, enroll as a citizen, and seek my own happiness by merging it in the communal felicity. At such times, utopia takes on a religious coloration; it seems the earthly counterpart of the Kingdom of Heaven. To hold back, to pose querulous questions is selfish and even blasphemous. And in these moods I ask myself whether I would not actually gain more freedom and scope for individuality than I lost. In the real America that I inhabit, how free am I? I am being constantly brainwashed by the sloganeers, not just those that sell soap or 200 per cent Americanism, but the more subtle sloganeers of a standardised and complacent liberalism. The ideas that seem most surely my own, the decisions I attribute only to myself — where do they come from? *The New York Times?* Conversations in the faculty lounge? The conditioning influences are so pervasive that most of the time I do not know they are there. But they shape me, as surely as a utopia shapes its people. If I enrolled in utopia, would the necessary degree of over-all planning and discipline, publicly carried out for the public good, really abridge my liberty as much as it is curtailed and conditioned every day in free America?

Such is one mood. At other times, in another mood, utopia leers. It seems not man's earnest effort to model his earthly affairs on the Kingdom of Heaven, but an impious attempt to create a rival kingdom, very much of this earth — one that subordinates individual selfishness only by converting it into the collective pride of the community, which then grows monstrous.

At still other times, utopia seems neither good nor bad, but simply a bore. I am haunted by Shakespeare. Could *Othello* ever have been written in a utopian society? Courtship and marriage are so sanely regulated that in utopian real-life an immature overgrown boy like Othello could not have secured permission to marry Desdemona. Or if he had, there would have been no Iago. The conditions of utopian life would not produce him, or if he appeared by some fluke, he would be promptly shipped off to a safely remote island. In a utopian world it is almost inconceivable that an Othello would ever smother a Desdemona. It seems wicked to say it, but this realisation comes to me with a sense of loss. Do I really want utopia if it means so perfect a world that there will be no real-life Othellos and Desdemonas to inspire the soaring and tragic verse of a Shakespeare?

Perhaps I have to make a choice: a just and happy society with much of the greatest literature rendered impossible by happiness, or an unjust, agonised, nasty society with an occasional Shakespeare or Dostoievski? Bellamy assures me that the perfect Boston of the future is producing much greater literature than the brutish old Boston had achieved. I wish I could see some samples of it. Until then I will suspect, though I cannot prove it, that great literature has a way of growing out of the dunghill of agony and suffering. All the modern Russian novels about happy tractor-drivers and workers who exceed production norms have done nothing to convince me that the rationally planned society will outdo Dostoievski in literary greatness.

As I have confessed, I say all these things with a guilty conscience. But in the mood I have been describing, utopia seems simply a virtuous bore. This mood is accurately captured by W. H. Auden in his poem, 'The Unknown Citizen: To JS/07/M/378 This Marble Monument Is Erected by the State':

He was found by the Bureau of Statistics to be
One against whom there was no official complaint,
And all the reports on his conduct agree
That, in the modern sense of an old-fashioned word, he
    was a saint,
For in everything he did he served the Greater Com-
    munity.
Except for the War till the day he retired
He worked in a factory and never got fired,
But satisfied his employers, Fudge Motors Inc.
Yet he wasn't a scab or odd in his views,
For his Union reports that he paid his dues,
(Our report on his Union shows it was sound)
And our Social Psychology workers found
That he was popular with his mates and liked a drink,
The Press are convinced that he bought a paper every day

And that his reactions to advertisements were normal in
every way.
Policies taken out in his name prove that he was fully in-
sured,
And his Health-card shows he was once in hospital but
left it cured.
Both Producers Research and High-Grade Living declare
He was fully sensible to the advantages of the Instalment
Plan
And had everything necessary to the Modern Man,
A phonograph, a radio, a car and a frigidaire.
Our researches into Public Opinion are content
That he held the proper opinions for the time of year;
When there was peace, he was for peace; when there was
war, he went.
He was married and added five children to the population.
Which our Eugenist says was the right number for a
parent of his generation,
And our teachers report that he never interfered with
their education.
Was he free? Was he happy? The question is absurd:
Had anything been wrong, we should certainly have
heard.

You have probably noticed a curious thing. I read this
poem to illustrate the boredom with which the idea of
utopia often afflicts me. But the poem doesn't deal with
utopia at all, but with the socially adjusted, tested and
measured society in which we now and increasingly live.
The Unknown Citizen does not step from the pages of
More or Wells. He is probably an other-directed worker in
Detroit.

This illutrates a final point. It is becoming difficult to
separate the utopian dream from contemporary reality.

68

The Composite Utopia

Much of utopia is coming true, piecemeal. Perhaps America, and not America alone, is nearer to utopia than we have realised.

If large parts of the world are indeed being remodelled into utopian shapes, this in itself helps to explain the growing numbers of dystopian novels. Utopia gleams less brightly when you have it. This is something we shall have to look into, later on.

CHAPTER SIX

The Dystopian Counter-attack

THE UTOPIAN vision is possible because utopian thinkers hold to a number of implicit presuppositions about the human condition. It is obvious that some assumptions rule out *a priori* any hope of utopia. If one believes in the simplest theory of the 'law of the jungle' and assumes man is for ever a ravening beast, concerned only with his own brute survival, there is no hope of utopia. Some types of Christian theology — those that picture us as irrational and sinful beings who can be 'saved' but not basically changed this side of the grave — also preclude utopia. The utopian dreamer must have grounds of hope, hope for the here and now. If he takes too dour a view of man's nature, the dream cannot exist.

It is fairly easy to deduce the principal articles of faith entertained by the utopian. One simply reads between the lines. Most utopian schemes assume the truth of the following statements, or at least most of them:

1. Man is basically good. H. G. Wells, in *A Modern Utopia*, makes this explicit: "The leading principle of the Utopian religion is the repudiation of the doctrine of original sin." Man's basic goodness doesn't mean he is good at every moment, or ever completely good; there may be a lot of the old ape or old Adam still in him. But his 'evil' can be eliminated or reduced to manageable proportions by a good environment, education, moral training, perhaps even by genetic controls.

2. Man is exceedingly plastic. His 'nature' is a fiction. Within very broad limits, at any rate, he can be shaped and conditioned to fit happily into whatever society one chooses to create. Some writers even consider directing the course of biological evolution, as in *Last and First Men*, where 'Martian units' are incorporated into the brain to provide a telepathic sense.

3. There is no need for a dichotomy between the happiness of the individual and that of society. In a really good society, a total happiness is achieved.

4. Man is a rational being and can become more so. His powers of reason can be harnessed to the task of creating a society that makes better sense than any existing society. There is nothing sacred about the social institutions that have so haphazardly evolved. Just as real science has supplanted a great mass of half-scientific, half-superstitious folk-lore, so a real science of society can create something much better than the accidental society now existing.

5. The future holds a finite number of possibilities, which can be sufficiently foreseen for practical purposes. The utopian planner need not worry about the outrageously unexpected event. Mankind has had sufficient experience to foresee the probable consequences of any course of action.

6. The purpose of utopia is man's earthly welfare. By implication, any other welfare — while not necessarily an illusion — is not the direct goal of utopia. (A warning at this point — this does not mean that utopia has to be 'materialistic', in the dollars-and-cents meaning of that word. Utopia is likely to emphasise cultural activities, altruism, education, and in general the 'finer things of life'. In the same way the 'materialism' of the Soviet Union is metaphysical rather than crudely centred on *things*, and it does not preclude an intense concern for culture.)

7. People don't get tired of happiness.

71

8. Rulers can be found who will rule justly, or men can be picked and trained so that they will rule justly. The danger of tyranny is slight, and can be reduced towards the vanishing point by education, wise selection, ascetic disciplines, or a few elementary checks and balances.

9. Utopia is not opposed to freedom. It will lead to 'true freedom', as individual men and women find their own destiny fulfilled by co-operating freely with the purposes of society.

I suppose the list could be further extended, but it will do for our purposes. Of the nine utopian articles of faith, the key ones are probably 1, 2 and 8 — the goodness of man, the plasticity of human nature, and the possibility of finding rulers who will not be corrupted by power. These are three mighty affirmations. Without them, the utopian venture could hardly be envisaged in the first place. Supported by some at least of the other assumptions, they provide a firm foundation on which the city of human dreams can be reared. The only question is: Is the foundation really firm? This is the question we shall have to ask constantly, as we explore the world of the dystopia.

The question has grown more urgent in this century, as one feature after another of utopia has been transferred from the drawing board to concrete social planning. We are compelled to ask — Do we really want utopia? The quotation from Nicolas Berdyaev which Aldous Huxley inserts at the beginning of *Brave New World* indicates the spirit in which the utopian dream is being re-evaluated:

Les utopies apparaissent comme bien plus réalisables qu'on ne le croyait autrefois. Et nous nous trouvons actuellement devant une question bien autrement angoissante: Comment éviter leur réalisation définitive? . . . Les utopies sont réalisables. La vie marche vers les utopies.

The Dystopian Counter-attack

Et peut-être un siècle nouveau commence-t-il, un siècle où les intellectuels et la classe cultivée rêveront aux moyens d'éviter les utopies et de retourner à une société non utopique, moins 'parfaite' et plus libre.

'Perhaps a new century will begin, a century in which the intellectuals and the cultivated classes will dream of how to avoid utopia and how to return to a non-utopian society, less perfect and freer.'

The anti-utopian reaction has been marked in this century, but it has existed from the start as a minor gadfly plaguing the utopian. Perhaps the Greeks, as usual, invented both the utopia and the dystopia. Plato's *The Republic* was hardly out of the scribe's hands before Aristophanes satirised it in his play, *The Ecclesiazusae*, which pokes fun at the system of sexual relations advocated by Plato and pictures an Athens ruled by women who have seized power in order to establish a communistic society free from crime and injustice.

Sometimes it is difficult to tell whether something is a dystopia or a rival utopia. For instance, the Christian dream of the Kingdom of God and still more its ascetic manisfestations, such as the monastic ideal, engendered a real-life opposite with a vast accompanying literature: the medieval cult of courtly love, in which the God of Love presided over a highly precise pattern of life, whose key feature was refined adultery. Should one say that the tales, poems and manuals celebrating this rival religion — which was not just a thing of the books, but a reality of boudoirs — were merely a satire on Christian asceticism? They were that at times, but also a positive ideal, with its own theology, casuistry, and discipline. Or what should one make of Rabelais' joyous Abbey? Again, the utopianism of the ascetic is attacked, but the Abbey is more than a satire. It is a utopia in its own right.

73

Thus one man's utopia may also be a dystopia to the person who has a different utopia.

The unambiguous dystopia seems to date from the 18th century, if one excludes occasional rare traces of it in earlier centuries. Fénelon's *Télémaque* provoked the anonymous *L'Île de Naudely* in satiric reaction. Swift, in *Gulliver's Travels*, provided not only a utopia of sorts in his land of the rational horses, but an unmistakable inverted utopia in Laputa, where crazy and impractical scientists try to run all mundane affairs in the spirit of pure mathematics.

The dystopia remained a minor irritant to the utopian until Bellamy wrote *Looking Backward*. This book so greatly appealed to many of his contemporaries, both in Europe and America, that they organised Bellamy societies and laid plans to create a socialist world on his model. The thing thus got into agitation and politics. Conservatives became alarmed, and their literary arm moved to the counter-attack. At the rate of about a book a year for the decade after *Looking Backward*, they produced novels dramatising the horrible consequences of Bellamy's theories. Most of these anti-utopias are superficial enough, and pay little attention to debating the fundamental assumptions of utopianism that I listed a moment ago. Their purpose is clear-cut and practical: they wish to expose socialism and defend *laissez-faire* capitalism.

Arthur Vinton's *Looking Further Backward* shrewdly combines a defence of capitalism with fears of the yellow peril. America has read Bellamy, gone socialist, and lost its stamina. China has had the good sense to resist the socialist sirens. Retaining its capitalistic virility, China invades the United States and easily conquers the demoralised socialists, deporting many of them to distant parts, and colonising the country with capitalistic Chinese.

Bellamy had many followers in Germany, and a number

The Dystopian Counter-attack

of the counter-attacks come from that direction. *Mr. East's Experiences in Mr. Bellamy's World*, by Konrad Wilbrandt, shows Bellamy socialism fully functioning in Berlin, with inefficiency, lowered productivity, loss of individual freedom, general stagnation. A more lurid counter-attack came from Philipp Wasserburg, writing under the pseudonym of Philipp Laicus. Entitled *Etwas Später!* and subtitled *Eine Fortsetzung von Bellamy's Rückblick aus dem Jahr 2000*, the novel has Cuba for its setting. The island has fallen under the influence of Bellamy's hero, Julian West, and has gone communistic, feministic, and atheistic. The horrors of communism are dramatised by the sight of a lazy patrician woman being disciplined at the whipping post to stimulate her enthusiasm for work. Apparently the solitary cell and bread and water had proved too mild.

Another anti-Bellamy book, Richard C. Michaelis's *Looking Forward*, uses the theory of evolution to vindicate the natural inequality of men, and confutes Bellamy's argument that the economic system is automatically evolving towards socialism. An interesting case of academic freedom is presented in the novel when a professor who has lectured on the merits of 19th-century capitalism is demoted to the rank of janitor.

One could cite many more of Bellamy's bastard offspring, but the foregoing examples give the general tenor of the counter-attack. As I have said, most of these books probe only superficially into the possibilities and perils of utopian planning. They are written with the conditioned reflexes of the conservative and read like the outraged cries of men who know, *know* in their bones, without further demonstration or debate, that socialism automatically leads to moral decay, loss of national stamina, decreased productivity, the death of chivalry and the denial of God. For more profound critiques of utopia we must look elsewhere.

75

From Utopia to Nightmare

The early 20th century saw a book by a Russian, Valerius Bruzov, that probes deeper. *The Republic of the Southern Cross* is more than an attack on economic and social theories; it says something about the enduring perversity of man's nature. The story describes a centre of world civilisation located at the South Pole, one of the countless glassed-in cities that both utopians and anti-utopians love to imagine. The metropolis is heated by electricity, and connected with outlying cities and towns by covered passageways. The economy is communistic, efficiently managed. The government is a benevolent autocracy. There are some distasteful features such as censorship and uniforms for all, as well as an early curfew, but nothing brutal or nightmarish. Everyone has cradle-to-grave security. There is free education, recreation, and medical care. The government even sponsors a suitable variety of religions, one for every temperament. The work span is only twenty years; the pensions are adequate. So what we have is a communist system functioning humanely and effectively. From all appearances it should endure for ever.

It does not. A mysterious ailment appears. For a time it crops up here and there; gradually it gets out of control. The disease, which no doctor can cure, is *Mania Contradiceus*. Its victims, whose numbers are constantly increasing, have an irresistible impulse to do the precise opposite of what is suggested to them. Conductors insist on paying their passengers. Topsy-turvy madness reigns. Furious quarrels arise from misunderstandings; society breaks asunder. Many people crack up under the tension and commit suicide. The entire utopian world becomes one vast asylum. At last the imperfect outside world compassionately comes to the rescue with aeroplanes, transporting the demented to a less ideal but somehow saner world, where they can recover.

The Republic of the Southern Cross does not read like the

The Dystopian Counter-attack

work of an old coupon-slipper, fearful that the industries in which he has invested will be nationalised. It is the work of a man who has dug deeper and caught some glimpses of the plain 'orneriness' which is at once man's shame and his glory. The book is an important pathbreaker for the inverted utopias that have formed such a distinct literary category since the First World War. It is concerned with some fundamental questions: Does man as a species have a definite 'nature'? Can that nature be changed? Can a society be rationally blueprinted and then created without doing violence to the stubborn human factor? How far can man shape his own destiny? Are there built-in limits to the scope of his planning? What is happiness? Does utopian planning lead to happiness? Is personal freedom a luxury or a necessity? Finally, are man's nature and the utopian dream locked in inescapable conflict, so that one or the other must yield? It is these more disturbing questions that the best of the later dystopias are also intent on exploring.*

* For further discussion of the anti-Bellamy reaction and 19th and early 20th century inverted utopias, see *Touring Utopia* by Frances Theresa Russell, and *Pilgrims Through Space and Time*, by J. O. Bailey.

CHAPTER SEVEN

Invitation to Inferno

A TRIP through the modern inverted utopias is a repetition of Dante's journey through hell, except that there are more than nine circles. We shall start with some of the upper ones, relatively tolerable for habitation, and progress towards the frozen centre. Our tour will of necessity be very selective. We shall by-pass certain of the circles altogether.

We have already seen how Bellamy provoked an outraged reaction, expressed in a series of anti-socialist replies to *Looking Backward*. Most of them are superficial, but they do at least pose the important question of whether socialist planning does or not inevitably entail a loss of liberty, and perhaps a decline in efficiency. The anti-socialist reaction is continued in the 20th century by a number of authors. One is Condé B. Pallen, widely known in his lifetime as a Roman Catholic journalist and writer. His one novel is *Crucible Island* (1919), depicting a socialist 'utopia' in which protest is treason, marriages are dictated by the state, and children are taught the Socialist catechism, which begins:

Q. By whom were you begotten?
A. By the Sovereign State.
Q. Why were you begotten?
A. That I might know, love, and serve the Sovereign State always.
Q. What is the Sovereign State?
A. The Sovereign State is Humanity in composite and perfect being.

78

Invitation to Inferno

Q. Why is the State supreme?

A. The State is supreme because it is my Creator and Conserver, in which I am and move and have my being and without which I am nothing.

Q. What is the individual?

A. The individual is only a part of the whole, and made for the whole, and finds his complete and perfect expression in the Sovereign State. Individuals are made for co-operation only, like feet, like hands, like eyelids, like the rows of the upper and lower teeth.

The anti-socialist reaction is continued by a much more distinguished writer, Evelyn Waugh. His short story, *Love Among the Ruins*, is written with a morose hatred of the advancing, semi-socialist welfare state in England. The action takes place in the near future. There is the familiar picture of general dinginess, inefficiency, sloppiness. The top officials of the government reveal by their speech that they have studied neither at Eton nor at Oxford. A slovenly sentimentality permeates all their actions. This is dramatised by the case of Miles, who becomes a national hero after setting fire to an air force base with great loss of life. He is sent to a magnificent house of correction, rather like a country manor, where the infinite understanding and kindness of the experts rehabilitates him. Since he is the first success of the new penology, he is precious in the eyes of the government and clearly destined for an illustrious career.

As a stopgap, until he can be placed in a post more suited to his talents, he is assigned to the Department of Euthanasia, the one enterprise now flourishing in the welfare state. Each morning the eager crowds line up waiting their turn for a whiff of cyanide. The numbers are becoming so unmanageable that there is serious talk of charging a fee to discourage the frivolous.

79

From Utopia to Nightmare

Soon Miles meets Clara. A ballet dancer, she has undergone the usual sterilisation operation, but by some surgical freak a full beard has resulted. She yearns for death, and applies for it. But beard or no beard, she is still beautiful. Without too much difficulty Miles persuades her to live and they become lovers. In spite of her operation, she is soon pregnant. But medical science comes to the rescue. She has an abortion and plastic surgery removes her beard, restoring her to the ballet stage and snatching her from Miles's embrace.

This depresses Miles, and in his state of depression he casually burns down the house of correction, with great loss of life. This time his deed is not discovered. At the end of the story he is offered an important job by the Minister of Rest and Culture, His task is to travel around, delivering public lectures on the new penology and modestly pointing to himself as its vindication. But there is one catch. '"Folks like a bloke to be spliced,"' the Minister explains. He introduces Miles to a hideously ugly girl. Miles acquiesces. The two go together to the registrar's office. During the wedding ceremony his mood changes again. He fidgets with his cigarette lighter, and a tiny flame bursts forth, 'gemlike, hymeneal, auspicious'.

Mr. Waugh's story is written with the acid bite one would expect from an author of his particular talents, and it has some telling touches. For instance, the new penology — so full of loving kindness towards criminals — can be ruthless to the common citizen, who is threatened with contempt of court if he complains too much at the lack of protection. This particular world of Waugh is a topsy-turvy land in which ministers of culture speak substandard English, the industry of death flourishes while all others stagnate, and criminals are national heroes. It is a protest against many of the tendencies current on both sides of the Atlantic — in

80

particular, against that soft kind of compassion that relieves men of moral responsibility.

Waugh's tale thus continues and elaborates the quarrel with modernity, socialist modernity in particular, that earlier anti-utopians had carried on. In this he does not stand alone. A very interesting writer, Ayn Rand, belongs in the same company, though a short story is too short for her. Recently to the fore in America as the lecture-circuit philosopher of conservative and more-than-conservative groups, Miss Rand sincerely believes that altruism is the bane of mankind. Creativity flowers when each person looks out for number one. Her nightmare is a world in which the incompetents exploit the conscience of their betters and impose a society tailored to their own mediocrity. She places her hopes in the rebels who discover their own ego and constitute a 'saving remnant' or 'creative minority', depending on whether one's vocabulary is biblical or Toynbeean.

Anthem is a work of only 105 pages. Published in 1954, it pictures the new society that emerges after the present one has smashed up. It is completely static. A committee determines your occupation for life, with no possibility of change. The various occupations even live in separate parts of town. The hero is a bright boy who asks too many questions, and is punished by being assigned to the ranks of the street sweepers for life. One day he explores a tunnel and discovers some old electrical equipment. He puts it together and secretly gets it to working. Wishing to share the rediscovery he goes to the philosophers, who are horrified that a mere street sweeper should concern himself with such things. Severe punishment confronts him. To escape, he disappears into a great forest that no one ever penetrates. There he encounters a girl whom he has previously met. The forest turns out to be beautiful and free of perils. The two of them keep going and come out on the other side. There they find an old house, still habitable. They decide to settle down. There is the implication that they will be the nucleus of a new and free society, which will be the saving remnant after the caste-ridden world of their past has been destroyed by its own psychological and social rigidities. The word they plan to carve over the portals of their fort is EGO. The book is written more like a prose poem or hymn to the Self than a mere novel; it has a greater impact than Waugh's brittle tale.

Atlas Shrugged (1957) is a humourless book of 1168 pages developing the same theme. This is America in the latter part of the 20th century. The government has taken over one activity after another in an ultra New Deal. There is general corruption on all levels and creeping inefficiency. One by one the great industrialists, frustrated beyond endurance, simply disappear. They flee to a hidden community in Colorado and establish an individualistic society which in time will be the hope of humanity.

So far we have been concerned with imaginary worlds in which the shackling of individual enterprise leads to inefficiency, drabness, the exploitation of the competent by the mediocre, and a general decline of society. These books, in short, are a protest against big government. (They are less concerned with the effective planning done informally by big business and cartels.) The protest against planning has been broadened out and stated in more profound and disturbing terms by other writers, whom we shall meet in the inferno's lower circles, but at least the anti-Bellamyites — and Waugh and Rand — do raise questions serious enough to merit the attention of anyone whose cast of mind inclines him towards favouring an increasing role for the government, its functionaries, and their electronic computers.

Before we visit the nether regions of hell, there are some

intermediate circles that should detain us a brief while. One circle is inhabited by machinery that turns against its master. Ever since the industrial revolution picked up steam, literally and figuratively, the imaginers of hypothetical worlds have divided over its merits. Bellamy and Wells were all out for the machine. Other writers to one degree or another have been haunted by a kind of Frankenstein legend, the fear that man's mechanical creations will master him. This may not involve anything so fanciful as the doings of the robots in Karel Čapek's play, *R.U.R.* Man can become enslaved to machines simply by being too dependent on them. William Dean Howells, in *A Traveller from Altruria* (1894) attempted to have the best of both worlds — handicrafts and the industrial age. Machinery is used for its brute power, but handicrafts are practised by the Altrurians as art and labour of love. William Morris in *News from Nowhere* (1890) pictures a revolutionary crowd smashing the machines and returning to the artistic standards of 14th-century handicrafts. They become so contented in consequence that the life-span lengthens and men age more slowly. Other anti-machine worlds are W. H. Hudson's *A Crystal Age* (1887) and Samuel Butler's *Erewhon, or, Over the Range* (1872).

Of the anti-machine dystopias, one of the most interesting is a long-short-story by E. M. Forster, *The Machine Stops*. The setting is some time in the future. The surface of the earth has been completely deserted by the human race. Mankind, having now lived for aeons in luxurious and gracious cities underground, is convinced that no one can survive on the skin of the globe without a respirator. On the rare occasions that anyone emerges from the long tunnels and takes an aeroplane trip the shades are carefully closed so that the passengers will not see the hideous surface of the old planet.

From Utopia to Nightmare

This underground world is beautifully organised. Machinery and society take care of everything. The rights of parents cease at birth; children are reared well in public nurseries. Work is done by the vast Machine that ramifies into every city and apartment; it even does most of the people's thinking. The official religion is Undenominational Mechanism.

It is a refined world. The human body, having little to do, is white and flabby. Handshaking is bad form. People rarely meet face to face; it is too crudely physical. Instead of going to public lectures, they listen to discourses over TV. When friends or relatives wish to meet, they usually have recourse to TV also. One cause of misunderstanding between Vashti and her son, Kuno, is that he actually wishes to visit her in her apartment. This seems very unspiritual to her.

Kuno is an atavistic throw-back. He believes in God rather than the Machine, and he sneaks away and visits the surface of the planet. For this he is in danger of being condemned to 'homelessness' — exile on the face of the earth, without benefit of respirator. Meanwhile the government, alarmed by unauthorised trips, abolishes all respirators, explaining that future lectures about the surface of the earth can be based on past lectures, and that this is really more intellectual than depending on fir:.t-hand observation.

When this world of infinite refinement and perfect organisation at last begins to break down, hardly anyone is aware of it for a time. True, the Machine is developing quirks. It doesn't function quite as smoothly as it used to. And it is true that no one knows how to repair it. It has never needed repairs. But for a time, there is little to worry about, except an occasional flickering of the lights. Then stranger things happen. Someone applies to the Machine for euthanasia and gets a garbled answer. One thing after another goes wrong, at an accelerating tempo. Panic begins to sweep the whole underground world. The clamour for euthanasia mounts. Then a moment comes when all the lights go out. The entire world is stampeded into madness. The people pour into the dark corridors and tunnels, and there in the madness and tumult they perish.

Once again, there is a saving remnant. At various times certain rebellious men and women have been condemned to 'homelessness' and banished to the surface. There they have discovered that, contrary to the teachings of science, they can breath without artificial aids. A new society has sprung up, primitive in many ways but virile and functioning. The future of mankind rests with it, now that the flabbily sensitive souls have miserably perished.

Several themes are obviously mingled in this story. One is the danger that men will become so dependent on machinery that it will in effect enslave them and finally destroy them by its own breakdown. Another theme is what Forster calls 'the sin against the body'. The underground people are pseudo-angels, trying to live like disembodied spirits. Their very refinement and spirituality weaken them to such an extent that when their environment changes — by the collapse of the Machine — they cannot adapt and survive.

It is easy to dismiss Forster's story as too fantastic. Our bodies, though seldom up to physical-education standards, are solidly with us and we prefer to live in penthouses rather than caverns. Nor has machinery quite reached the point that the author depicts. Thus one's first reaction is that the tale is pretty far-fetched. And yet, second thoughts occur. It may be later than we think. Perhaps machinery has been biding its time, and is now at the point of taking over, not precisely in Forster's way, but just as irrevocably.

The machinery-*v.*-man theme is developed with a different twist in *Player Piano: America in the Coming Age of*

From Utopia to Nightmare

Electronics (1952), by Kurt Vonnegut, Jr. This novel shows America in the fairly near future, after the second industrial revolution, the electronic one, has triumphed. Mr. Vonnegut's picture is all the more appalling because he does not smear the canvas with horrors. Many things in his future America have not changed at all. There is no dictatorship, no secret police with rubber truncheons or steel whips. The general fabric of democracy and freedom is preserved intact. Thanks to automatic machinery, there is a fantastic increase in productivity, so that the problem of poverty is at last solved once and for all. Also, wars have ceased. At first glance, it mounts up to an authentic utopia.

But it is utopia only for people with very high I.Q.s. They are spotted early, sent to graduate and engineering schools, and trained to be the new *élite*. The average man finds less and less to do. The old assembly line is run by electronic devices; a whole factory requires only a handful of beautifully trained experts. The unemployed have two choices — enlist in the army, now useless, for a twenty-five-year hitch and retire on a good pension, or lean on a shovel with the 'Reeks and Wrecks' (Reconstruction and Reclamation Corps). It isn't that anyone physically suffers. Productivity is so high that even the unemployed have the necessities of life and some modest luxuries. But products accumulate and men decay. This is a world with no meaning and no future for anyone with an I.Q. under 140.

The routine affairs of the new America are run by computers and I.B.M. machines, which operate with an inhuman perfection. In a periodic check of government employees, the machines discover that one high official never completed his physical education requirement in college. In order to validate his degrees, he must make up the deficiency. Fat, puffing and middle-aged he returns to his Alma Mater to be confronted by the wrathful director of physical education,

86

who resents some remarks recently made about the undue stress on athletics. The result is a series of physical tests impossible to pass.

The unemployed and useless indulge in daydreams about the good old days of the assembly line, when a man felt useful. Their resentment and frustration arouses sympathy in some of the more sensitive engineers, who are horrified at the social fruits of their ingenuity. There is a rebellion, a spate of machine smashing. But it is half-hearted from the start, and soon ends. Before long, the rebels begin searching among the ruins, rescuing bits of electronic equipment and rebuilding the very machines that have rendered them superfluous. The Machine seems to have become a habit-forming drug. Humanity can't live with it or without it — such is the ironic moral of a novel that is peculiarly disturbing because it is so plausible, so matter-of-fact.

I find it impossible to discuss *Player Piano* in a vacuum. The book reads like the headlines of day after tomorrow. Anyone who stays a while in Detroit can sense the anxieties produced by the quiet growth of automation. The American newspapers already carry disquieting items. One learns that employment in certain widely scattered industrial centres remains unnaturally low even though business and productivity have picked up and reached new heights. The labour unions are becoming conscious of automation, and intent on including some consideration of its effects in their negotiations. Perhaps, as Vonnegut believes, we are just at the beginning of the second industrial revolution; perhaps automation is taking over so quietly and discreetly that at first hardly anything seems to be changed, except a little pocket of persistent unemployment here and there, and quite heavy unemployment among the poorly educated. But if the second industrial revolution comes in full force, it will not be a mere intensification of the first. The first moved the peasant, the hired hand, and the small-scale craftsman from the farm or home workshop to the factory and its machines. The second industrial revolution will move the assembly-line worker to — nothing. Nothing, except charity or make-believe work. A new world may be dawning in which the stupid or the untrained and uneducated will serve no purpose, and if they continue to eat and breathe, it will be as the wards of a compassionate society.

One continues to speculate. It is as though *Player Piano* projects the newsreel of the day after tomorrow. If the mass of men and women who do routine factory and clerical work are thrown out of employment, what next? A few could become small businessmen. A fair number might go into services — taking care of public parks, working as orderlies in hospitals, etc. Perhaps the servant problem would be solved — as it is in Michael Young's *The Rise of the Meritocracy*, when the technologically unemployed become the servants of the new *élite*. It is intriguing to imagine the scientists and engineers living in hierarchal splendour, with large retinues of butlers, cooks, gardeners, maids, and ever-ready baby-sitters. But even this could not take care of all the unemployed. So what next? If Vonnegut is right, national productivity will be such that the unemployed will eat well. What will suffer is not their bodies but their self-respect. Can the men whose sensibilities have been dulled by years on the assembly line and years of evenings in the tavern or pool hall suddenly profit from their leisure by turning to arts and crafts, or reading Bertrand Russell? It would be reassuring to think so.

So much for this excursion into real life and the plausible shape of things to come in the great industrial nations. Now for another look at real life. I earlier mentioned the theme of over-refinement or over-spirituality, the desire to be as the angels, which characterised the people of Forster's underground cities. This theme, common in the dystopias, reflects and magnifies certain facts of today's reality, as well as an element of utopian yearning. In real life, American at least, there is a curious cult of euphemism among a people who pride themselves on plain talking. Loved ones (not corpses) lie in slumber-rooms for a last *rendezvous* with their friends; rose petals and not earth are strewn over the casket; they are buried in graves over which no vertical stone will ever arise lest it suggest a cemetery. In the face of death we turn to euphemism both of word and deed.

In the village of Wellesley, the tract of land that I should call a city dump was labelled 'land fill area'. Soaps, toothpastes, perfumes and shaving lotions ensure that no American need smell in the least like humanity. These are minor things, perhaps. But they point towards a finicky desire to deny our crude, creaturely, physical reality.

In the utopias there is often a tidying-up of both the natural and human scene, with much emphasis on spick-and-span; more wordage is given to edifying lectures at meal-time than to what is on the table. The desire to be as the angels attains an appropriate symbolism in *Limanora, the Island of Progress* (1903), a utopia by Godfrey Sweven, who in his daily life was John Macmillan Brown, chancellor of the University of New Zealand. His imaginary citizens shun any contact with animals or 'degenerate or undeveloped men', for fear of being debased by the proximity. They are working hard to find some means of reproduction other than sex; already they have succeeded in reducing sex to its purely reproductive function, so that the Limanorans can now wear transparent garments — solely as protection against heat and cold — without offence to modesty. Symbolically enough, these remarkable beings, who have advanced so far towards angelhood, have acquired wings and flit about in a state of gleaming innocence. Even H. G.

Wells, who never devalued sex in either real life or fiction, is concerned to clean up the landscape by ridding it of most animal life, except the picturesque creatures or those that make good pets.

Not all utopias are afflicted with angelism, but it is sufficiently frequent to deserve note. In the inverted utopias, angelism often becomes a main feature. Forster's *The Machine Stops* dramatises the 'sin against the body' and its calamitous consequences. The theme of false and fatal spirituality or over-refinement is prominent on Franz Werfel's dystopia, *Star of the Unborn* (1946). This long and lumbering novel delineates the very distant future. Even Nature has become refined. Through some cosmic development, the garish green grass has been supplanted by grey turf; birds have long since perished, yielding to large butterflies. Mankind has gone underground and lives in circumstances of exquisite refinement. People seem almost bodiless. Their food is delicate liquids. Handshaking, once again, is tabu. Upper-class women are usually capable of producing only one child; more is considered vulgar. Death is sweetened by a form of voluntary euthanasia, whose appurtenances suggest the sentimental evasions of a first-class California cemetery. Those who feel they have lived long enough go to a vast underground Place, the Wintergarden, where they are subjected to the process of retrovolution. They shrink in size and mentality, repassing the stages of youth and babyhood, and turn then into a foetus and finally a kind of seed which is carefully planted in the subterranean garden to grow into an immortal daisy. Symbolically and significantly, the process of retrovolution is perilous. There is always a percentage of failures — persons who retrovolve only to a point and remain for ever in an agonised in-between state, about the size of carrots and still faintly human in appearance.

While the underground world has been enjoying its elegant tranquillity, strange patches of jungle have sprung up here and there on the surface, as though the crude energies of nature were regrouping for a counter-attack. These jungles are inhabited by a vigorous if somewhat primitive folk, who resemble the conventional picture of Balkan mountaineers. A war accidentally breaks out between the two peoples. The undergrounders cannot face confusion, uncertainty and danger. By droves they take the easy way out — to the Wintergarden. Once more the future is left to the sturdy, crude people of the surface. "*L'homme n'est ni ange ni bête,*" Pascal said. The moral in this novel, as in *The Machine Stops,* seems to be that when people play at being angels they will perish more miserably than the beasts.

CHAPTER EIGHT

The Frozen Depths of the Inferno

THE DEEPER circles of the Inferno display most of the better known dystopias. Probably the most famous of all, and certainly one of the most perfect from a literary viewpoint, is Aldous Huxley's *Brave New World*. Published in 1932, it is still widely read all over the world.

Brave New World is a picture of the world six hundred years from now, but Mr. Huxley, in a foreword to a later edition, revises the estimate and predicts that a century may be sufficient for the triumph of happiness-engineering, the basic control device in the society of the Brave New World.

This novel draws its inspiration and derives its nightmares not from the misdeeds of fascists or communists but from the popular culture of America. It is a satire not so much on the literary utopias as on the popular utopian yearnings of the average man, who wants nothing so much as to be happy. The small group of intellectuals controlling the world have discovered that happiness and social stability are perfectly feasible, so long as freedom is eliminated. What no society can have is all three. *Brave New World* shows how happiness and stability can be scientifically produced.

To ensure happiness, it is necessary first of all that no one be bored at his work. Dull work must be done by dull people; very dull work by very dull people. The problem has been solved by prenatal conditioning. Conventional motherhood, with its haphazard results, is now obsolete. All births (decantings) take place in state hatcheries. The future Alphas are permitted to develop normally. Lower castes — they range down to Epsilon Minuses — are given special treatment to stunt their brains in varying degrees, so that their mental development will tally with the work they have been predestined to do. The future lift operator will find each descent or ascent of the lift an exciting challenge to his meagre intelligence.

As a further guarantee against discontent, the science of hypnopaedia has been highly developed. A child, asleep in the public nurseries, hears all night long a voice whispering, telling him how lucky he is to be a Beta, a Gamma, whatever he is.

One particularly happy scientific break-through is Bokanovsky's Process, by which one human egg can be made to divide and subdivide. Sometimes, when maximum success is achieved, as many as ninety-six identical babies can be produced from one egg — enough to staff a small factory.

The majority of women are prenatally sterilised. The others are taught the most efficient methods of contraception, until the technique becomes a conditioned reflex. The word 'mother' is an obscenity. The old habit of associating the words love, marriage, sex, parenthood, child-rearing is completely lost and now incomprehensible. Love, as understood by the ancient romantics, no longer exists. Sex is free and easy and officially encouraged.

It is, in fact, hard to say where sex ends and religion begins. The devotions of *Brave New World* resemble the ancient fertility cults, except that they have nothing to do with fertility. Its people are a religious folk. Invoking Our Ford (sometimes called Our Freud) and making the sign of the model T, and with a dating system B.F. and A.F., they assemble every other week for a solidarity service. It is conducted as follows. The worshippers meet in small rooms,

93

twelve to a group, equally divided by sex. The loving cup of strawberry ice-cream *soma* is passed around as a kind of eucharist; *soma* is a harmless narcotic, producer of beautiful visions, and essential to the happiness of the people, who are taught to say, "Better a gramme than a damn." As each person quaffs from the cup he intones, in the grand language of mysticism, "I drink to my annihilation." Next, the First Solidarity Hymn is sung:

> Ford, we are twelve; oh make us one,
>> Like drops within the Social River;
> Oh, make us now together run
>> As swiftly as thy shining Flivver.

Twelve stanzas in all. Then the loving cup again. Drums begin to beat. Another hymn is sung:

> Come, Greater Being, Social Friend,
>> Annihilating Twelve-in-One!
> We long to die, for when we end,
>> Our larger life has but begun.

Another twelve stanzas.

The presence of the Greater Being becomes felt in the room. There is more singing, and a ritualistic dance, each person beating out the rhythm on the buttocks of the person ahead of him. "Ford!" cry the worshippers. A voice booms out the song:

> Orgy-porgy, Ford and fun.
> Kiss the girls and make them One.
> Boys at one with girls at peace;
> Orgy-porgy gives release.

Gradually the worshippers, pair by pair, retire to the convenient couches and consummate their worship, to the crooning tune of 'Orgy-Porgy'.

The Frozen Depths of the Inferno

Other evidences of progress in *Brave New World* are the 'feelies', which add a new dimension of realism to the cinema, and special hospitals for the dying where all the comforts of *soma* and incessant TV are provided. Parties of children are brought to gape at the patients and are given special treats afterwards, so that their thoughts of mortality will be ice-cream flavoured.

The economy of *Brave New World* is based on wasteful consumption. To keep the factories humming, people must consume even when they don't really want or need to. There is constant propaganda to increase consumption, and the population is encouraged to play games that require the most complicated and expensive equipment.

As I have already implied, the Brave New World is a static society. Science brought it into existence, but now science itself, with its new discoveries, may become a disruptive threat. All discoveries and inventions are strictly censored by the government, which files away the great majority with no intention of ever releasing them. It has been found, for instance, that the work day could be drastically reduced by technological advances, but a small-scale experiment has demonstrated that this would lead only to undue use of *soma*; it is obvious that labour-saving devices must be introduced with the greatest caution.

It is a happily brainwashed world. Thanks to prenatal and postnatal conditioning, happiness-engineering, and the lack of disturbing and difficult challenges, the Brave New World has a greater stability than ancient China. Time has had a stop; history has ceased. One generation after another is decanted, reared by the loving state, put to its appointed tasks. The work is light, the routine of life is sweetened by *soma*, sex and sports. Death is no terror. It has lost its terror with its dignity. The Brave New World is a society that

95

has entered into a ghastly, this-worldly parody of the Eternal Now.

Not that happiness-engineering and the most dedicated social planning can eliminate the theoretical possibility of discontent and disorder. If the Alphas are going to function with top intelligence, their minds have to be left unmutilated. There is always the chance that they will experience strange longing and unrest, and cause trouble. Society, however, has created its methods for handling these little crises. If an Alpha becomes too unhappy or critical, he is gently spirited away to a distant island reserved for kindred souls. There he can carry on Platonic dialogues and be harmless.

The other threat to the Brave New World would be from the outside. Mr. Huxley does not import the Martians, but his world still has reservations of 'savages', and these are 'outsiders'. Mr. Savage comes from such a reservation, where he has grown up in superstition and squalor but has also acquired some familiarity with a forgotten author, Shakespeare. When he is brought into the Brave New World he creates a twitter of excitement with his fanatical worship of God, and his peculiar attitude towards women, whom he prefers modest. But he is only a nine days' wonder. Brave New World conquers. He hangs himself and the eternal society of happy people continues in its Eternal Now, without tragedy and without history.

In his foreword to the later edition (1946) of *Brave New World* Mr. Huxley, now a convert to the 'perennial philosophy', says:

. . . it seems worth while at least to mention the most serious defect in the story, which is this. The Savage is offered only two alternatives, an insane life in Utopia, or the life of a primitive in an Indian village, a life more human in some respects, but in others hardly less queer and

96

abnormal. At the time the book was written this idea, that human beings are given free will in order to choose between insanity on the one hand and lunacy on the other, was one that I found amusing and regarded as quite possibly true.

Huxley then goes to say that if he were writing the book today, he would include a third alternative* — a co-operative community of people, exiles and refugees from the Brave New World, and living somewhere on the Indian Reservation:

> In this community economics would be decentralist and Henry-Georgian, politics Kropotkinesque co-operative. Science and technology would be used as though, like the Sabbath, they had been made for man, not (as at present and still more so in the Brave New World) as though man were to be adapted and enslaved to them. Religion would be the conscious and intelligent pursuit of man's Final End, the unitive knowledge of the immanent Tao or Logos, the transcendent Godhead or Brahman. And the prevailing philosophy of life would be a kind of Higher Utilitarianism, in which the Greatest Happiness principle would be secondary to the Final End principle — the first question to be asked in every contingency of life being: 'How will this thought or action contribute to, or interfere with, the achievement, by me and the greatest possible number of other individuals, of man's Final End?'

In *Brave New World Revisited,* a book-length essay, Mr. Huxley argues that happiness-engineering is steadily on the march and the nightmare of the future will be closer to *Brave New World* than to *Nineteen Eighty-Four.* He cites as evidence the replacement of Stalin by Khrushchev. Terror

* He has since presented it in his recent novel, *Island.*

has partially yielded to blandishments, jolly-good-fellow-ism, and adroit happiness-engineering. Huxley seems to envisage four possibilities for mankind: the squalor and superstition of the Reservation (less and less possible, as the world becomes one world), the demonic nightmare of Orwell's novel (not as probable as one might think, for terror is an inefficient form of rule), the perpetual smile of *Brave New World* (the most likely), and, as an outside possiblity if men choose to be rational, a society co-operating soberly and rationally for the achievement of man's Final End, the unitive knowledge of the Tao.

The happiness engineers in *Brave New World* function quietly, compassionately and without inflicting pain on the objects of their solicitude. A world whose happiness, if you can call it that, is more ruthlessly engineered is presented by the Russian writer, Eugene Zamiatin, whose *We* — though startlingly similar to *Nineteen Eighty-Four* — antedates it by more than two decades and is much less familiar to the general reader.

The reasons for the relative obscurity of *We* lie in the author's life and his relation to the Russian Revolution.* Zamiatin was busy in the revolutionary movement during Tsarist days and endured the usual imprisonment and banishment. When the day of revolution at last came, he greeted it with boundless enthusiasm and proclaimed its promise in one lecture hall after another. But soon he began to take alarm at the course of events. This was still during the time of the comparatively humane Lenin, and the horrors of Stalinism lay in the invisible future, but already the drift towards totalitarianism was evident to one as acutely sensitive as Zamiatin. His growing anxieties led him to write *We*

* For a brief account of Zamiatin, see the introduction (Peter Rudy), foreword (Gregory Zilboorg), and preface (Marc Slonim) to the recent paperback edition of Eugene Zamiatin, *We*, E. P. Dutton & Co., Inc., New York.

in 1920 as a warning. It was never published in Russia, of course, but somehow the manuscript was smuggled abroad. An English translation was published in the United States in 1924, followed by versions in other languages. In time a Russian version was circulated — outside Russia.

In the late twenties the usual yelping pack of communist critics opened up on Zamiatin. *We* had never been distributed, at least legally, in Russia; the public libraries now stopped the circulation of his other books. In 1931 Zamiatin wrote to Stalin, curtly asking permission to leave the Soviet Union. The permission was granted. The exile went to Paris, wrote nothing else of importance once his Russian roots were severed, and died in 1937.

The narrator of *We*, who tells the story in the form of a personal journal, is an engineer, D-503, who is building a gigantic spaceship to carry the blessings of the perfect society to the most distant planets. (Men are known by numbers with consonants prefixed; women have a vowel plus a number.) The time is a thousand years in the future. The world is now the United State (no *s*). It is dotted with carefully planned cities, each surrounded by a high green wall to cut off any contact with untamed nature and the hairy survivors of a less organised life who still persist in the forests. Within the cities even the weather has been tamed. The sky is always clear and blue; there is never any thunder and lightning.

The ruler is called the Well-Doer. On ceremonial occasions he operates the Machine, by which criminals are publicly executed in a scene of elaborate ritual. The most serious crime is disloyal thought or action; this is regarded not merely as a breach of the laws, but as sacrilege against the sacred state and its holy ruler. Periodically the Well-Doer is re-elected on the well-named Day of Unanimity.

If the weather is under control, the inhabitants — wearing

number-plates and garbed in blue uniforms — are still more predictable. Their activities are controlled by a table of hours. Their happiness is ensured by the abolition of practically all freedom. The walls of their rooms are of glass to facilitate the benign supervision maintained by the Well-Doer and his spies. Even the streets are bugged with microphones to pick up the most casual conversations. Sex is strictly regulated, though there is one minor concession to privacy: the shades may be pulled down during sexual hours. Sexual relations are channelled through a central bureau. A person desiring sexual intercourse receives a pink ticket which entitles him to any person of the opposite sex, on the ethical principle that one belongs to all and all to one. But sex is one thing, and motherhood quite another. Only women who meet the maternal norm may become mothers. Part of the story concerns poor little O–90, ten centimetres short of the norm, who so badly wants a baby that she insists on having it, even though she knows she will perish under the Machine or be tortured to death in the huge glass bell from which the oxygen is slowly exhausted.

The ideal of life is to become as much like a machine as possible. Men try to walk and work like machines; robots serve as teachers; music is composed by a machine that turns out three sonatas per hour.

Part of the impact of *We* comes from the reader's realisation more than forty years later that this man was no mean prophet. Writing when the Soviet Union was almost at a pre-industrial and pre-scientific stage, he predicted the building of the first spaceship. He accurately forecast many of the nastier practices that have become standard in the police states of both the left and the right. His grasp of the totalitarian psychology is advanced and uncanny.

The story itself is the familiar one of an attempted rebellion against the all-powerful state. At the beginning,

The Frozen Depths of the Inferno

D–503 is ecstatically happy at his work on the spaceship, and his adulation of the Well-Doer is up to any norm. But he becomes involved with I–330, a woman of strong character and disturbing charm, who is secretly in touch with the wild men and women outside the green wall.

Initially D–503, though intrigued by I–330, can make nothing of her, except that she has an alarming allure for him. His mind has been shaped by the elegant precision of mathematics. The erratic and imprecise character of human emotions perplexes and torments him; he cannot reduce them to mathematics. But, almost in spite of himself, he finds himself involved in an affair with I–330, and through her he is plunged into revolutionary activities. For a brief while it looks as though the alliance between those inhabitants of the city who are discontented and the wild men outside will be successful. But the United State is saved by a last-minute break-through in medical research. An announcement appears on the front page of the *State Journal*:

REJOICE!

For from now on we are *perfect*!

Until today your own creation, engines, were more perfect than you.

WHY?

For every spark from a dynamo is a spark of pure reason; each motion of a piston, a pure syllogism. Is it not true that the same faultless reason is within you?

The philosophy of the cranes, presses, and pumps is complete and clear like a circle. But is your philosophy less circular? The beauty of a mechanism lies in its immutable, precise rhythm, like that of a pendulum. But have you not become as precise as a pendulum, you who are brought up on the system of Taylor?

Yes, but there is one difference:

MECHANISMS HAVE NO FANCY.

Did you ever notice a pump cylinder with a wide, distant, sensuously dreaming smile upon its face while it was working? Did you ever hear cranes that were restless, tossing about and sighing at night during the hours designed for rest?

NO!

Yet on your faces (you may well blush with shame!) the Guardians have more and more frequently seen those smiles, and they have heard your sighs. And (you should hide your eyes for shame!) the historians of the United State have all tendered their resignations as to be relieved from having to record such shameful occurrences.

It is not your fault; you are ill. And the name of your illness is:

FANCY.

It is a worm that gnaws black wrinkles on one's forehead. It is a fever that drives one to run farther and farther, even though 'farther' may begin where happiness ends. It is the last barricade on our road to happiness.

Rejoice! This Barricade Has Been Blasted at Last! The Road is Open!

The latest discovery of our State science is that there is a centre for fancy — a miserable little nervous knot in the lower region of the frontal lobe of the brain. A triple treatment of this knot with X-rays will cure you of fancy.

For ever!

You are perfect, you are mechanised; the road to one-

hundred-per-cent happiness is open! Hasten then all
of you, young and old, hasten to undergo the Great
Operation! Hasten to the auditoriums where the Great
Operation is being performed! Long live the Great
Operation! Long live the United State! Long live the
Well-Doer!

D–503 is finally compelled to undergo the operation, and
it has the promised effect. He is cured of restlessness and
imagination. He will be happy and good for ever. The next
day he appears before the Well-Doer and freely tells him
everything he knows about the rebellion. The same evening
he sits at the table with him and chats while I–330 is brought
in and placed inside the glass bell. In an absent and impersonal way he notes that — despite repeated torture — she
refuses to talk. But other rebels subjected to the bell do talk.
"Tomorrow they will all ascend the steps to the Machine of
the Well-Doer," he muses. "No postponement is possible,
for there still is chaos, groaning, cadavers, beasts in the
Western section; and to our regret there are still quantities
of Numbers who have betrayed Reason." His mind wanders
on tranquilly: "I hope we win. More than that; I am certain
we shall win. For Reason must prevail."

And so the story ends. The United State is entering into
eternal triumph. Just as the hatcheries in Huxley's *Brave New
World* cut down the oxygen ration of lower-caste embryos
so as not to handicap them with intelligence, so the United
State, by perfecting its mass-production lobotomy, has
surgically removed the restlessness from mankind and ensured an eternity of social adjustment, obedience and happiness. The old dream of Dostoievky's Grand Inquisitor (who
must be the patron saint of the dystopias) has been technically implemented; men have now permanently gained happiness by permanently losing their freedom.

We is one of many inverted utopias inspired by the

totalitarian movements of our century. It happens to use as its springboard a despotism of the left. Others have chosen some kind of fascism as their starting point. The 1930's and early 1940's produced abundant literary nightmares, such as Sinclair Lewis's *It Can't Happen Here*, showing what would happen if a democratic country went Nazi. But the actual prototype was so monstrous that there was little of interest that the writers could do to embellish it with additional horrors. Nazism was from the start the political philosophy of grown men acting like little boys pretending to be the Stone Age savages they had read about in comic books. Its ideals were those of the unthinking tribe, the blood rites, the dripping meat of the evening feast around the flaring fire. Communism has many advantages as a springboard for the dystopian. The Russian Revolution in theory and to some extent in practice incorporates a great deal of Western enlightenment and humanism. It has a doctrine of human brotherhood and justice, and it does not divide mankind into superior and inferior races. Thus any corruption of the communist dream, while not exactly a *corruptio optimi*, is at least a *corruptio boni*, and has a significance that the various stages of fascism and nazism could not possess. Zamiatin and others like him are warning us not against the horrible consequences of a political theory wicked and stupid from the start, but against the enormities that can rise from a relatively good movement when it becomes twisted, perverted and demonic.

This is a good point to mention one other book that seems to stem partially from the Russian experience, though one cannot pin it down and say that it is a satire on any one country or revolution. It is a novel distinguished by a high literary quality and characters who have some reality and psychological depth — literary luxuries in both the utopia and dystopia.

The Frozen Depths of the Inferno

The author of this book, *Bend Sinister*, is Vladimir Nabokov, now better known for *Lolita*. The English translation appeared shortly after the end of World War II. The central character is a world-famous professor of philosophy in some country that seems vaguely Slavic. He is a hard-bitten, stubborn, proud man, contemptuous of Paduk, the dictator, whom he knew in school by the nickname of Toad. Paduk has come to power through popularising the philosophy of a tower-of-ivory scholar, who, writing some time back, had insisted that a definite amount of consciousness exists in the world and justice requires its even distribution. This philosophy, Ekwilism, was a speculative thing with no social programme, but Paduk has been able to offer a concrete implementation — pretty much the standard dystopian gospel of group life and the joyful subordination of the individual.

Paduk wants Krug, the professor, to become president of the University. Krug resists. At last he is arrested and his young son spirited away. Krug is now ready to give in to save the boy. But it turns out that through a clerical error the boy has been turned over to a group of criminals who are being psychologically rehabilitated by letting them express their aggressions through tormenting the orphans entrusted to them. The son has been sadistically killed by one of the criminals. When Krug learns this, he goes berserk and is finally shot down.

This particular inverted utopia has no fantastic details about new inventions or radical surgery. Its peculiar horror arises from the plausibility of the world it presents and the psychological depth in the treatment of Krug — whose struggle reveals that even the strongest cannot stand up against this kind of tyranny and survive. There is a pervading smell of evil in the book, the feeling that demonic powers and principalities control this world, and that the familiar decencies and moral principles have, in the name of 'justice', been transvalued, so that goodness is cruelty and cruelty is goodness.

I come now to an inverted utopia that, like *Brave New World*, has become almost required reading in schools and universities. It has as valid a claim as any for occupying the narrow space in the bottom circle of hell. George Orwell's *Nineteen Eighty-Four*, published in 1949, is the work of a man whose reputation has had a steady and, in some ways, a curious rise since his death. He was no path-breaker in literary techniques; his novels read more like Dickens than Proust or Joyce. He had no startlingly new ideas about anything. Naturally sympathetic to the underdog, he could not be permanently attracted by communism; its hard, dogmatic, self-righteous face repelled him. His vision of the good life was a simple one — a world in which people could live in moderate comfort, talk freely without fear of electronic devices, make love when they chose to, and in general mind their own business and let others mind theirs. He wanted to remedy the grosser social injustices, but not at the price of turning men into happy — or unhappy — ants in an anthill. None of the glittering and blood-stained 'ism's of the century fitted him. The more he observed the world scene, the more he became certain that the dogmatists of the left had betrayed the ordinary man as surely as the dogmatists of the right.

It is the lack of dogmatism and ideology in the mature Orwell, and his simple re-affirmation of the most ordinary freedoms and decencies that marks his later work and is, one suspects, the main reason for the growth of what is now an Orwell cult. He is *not* a great writer, though he is a good one. But he did hold fast to a steady vision of the human being as an end in himself, an end more important than any social blueprint. He trusted his intuitions. Today, the disillusioned dogmatists of the left (and perhaps to some extent those of the right) find in him a balance and sanity that they need and seek.

Nineteen Eighty-Four is something close to the composite dystopia. Most of the horrors that other books have predicted are here combined and synthesised into 100 per cent nightmare. Even happiness, apart from the occasional pleasure of sadism, has disappeared from the lives of all except the degraded Proles, who don't count. Unlike the men and women of *We*, who got about with robot-like movements bespeaking a robot-like contentment, the inhabitants of *Nineteen Eighty-Four* are drab and cheerless. Orwell's book has a further distinction — he makes his points with a minimum of gimmicks. There is no decanting, no prenatal conditioning, no mass lobotomies. *Nineteen Eighty-Four* is feasible with our present science and technology.

The novel is primarily an extrapolation of Stalinism, though its purpose is broader than that. It pictures a globe that has gone completely totalitarian, in metaphysics as well as in political organisation. The earth is divided into three huge states, two of which are constantly at war with the third. The alliances shift overnight to avoid any chance of victory, which might lead to peace, an increase of social discontent and trouble for the three dictators.

It is a dingy world, rundown and inefficient in everything except the exercise of power. Science is stagnant; the only lines of research encouraged by the three governments are military weapons, brainwashing, and methods of mind-reading.

Sadistic brutality is no longer merely a political necessity, but a satisfaction in its own right, whose image is the boot eternally on the helpless face. Power is the supreme joy, almost the only one, and the way to feel powerful is to inflict pain on those who cannot escape it.

The power of Big Brother is exercised in every conceivable way. For example, the history of the past is at his mercy and that of the Party bosses. When the Party line changes, as it frequently does, all old issues of newspapers are destroyed in libraries and replaced by completely new ones, complete with the original dates. Thus anyone doing research will find not the authentic past but the past that suits Big Brother's purposes of the moment.

In every way the past fares poorly. Most of its literature, being subversive, is suppressed. The small part that is saved is being translated into a kind of Basic English called Newspeak, a tongue with an extreme simplicity of grammar and a constantly diminishing vocabulary. The purpose of Newspeak is not to make the expression of all ideas possible, but to render the expression of most ideas impossible for want of words; literally *unthinkable*. The Declaration of Independence, with its talk of truths, inalienable rights and liberty could not be translated into Newspeak. It could only be summarised by the expressive word, *crimethink*. On the other hand, Newspeak is capable of great emotional and poetic nuances in praising the new order and denouncing its enemies. Where a leader in the old (London) *Times* might laboriously assert, 'Those whose ideas were formed before the Revolution cannot have a full emotional understanding of the principles of English Socialism', Newspeak can say the same thing with admirable concision, 'Old thinkers unbellyfeel Ingsoc'.

Newspeak is the Orwellian equivalent of a lobotomy. It deprives men of the words by which they can think connected and rational thoughts and communicate them. At the period of the book Oldspeak and Newspeak are both current, but Newspeak is rapidly gaining and will soon be the only language. When that time comes, a man may still feel emotions of discontent and resentment, but he will not be able to analyse them — analysis requires words — nor share his feeling with others. If there is no word for *freedom*, how can men conspire and fight and die for it? How can they even know it is what they want?

Closely allied to Newspeak is the official metaphysical system, Doublethink, which enables its followers to hold two contradictory ideas simultaneously. Its subtleties are indicated by the four departments of the government. The Ministry of Peace wages war. The Ministry of Truth distributes propaganda. The Ministry of Plenty supervises rationing. The Ministry of Love operates the torture chambers. The other characteristic of the metaphysical system is an extreme and consistent collective solipsism — there is no abstract or eternal truth. Whatever the Party says is true *is* true, as long as the Party says it. It ceases to be true when the Party ceases to assert it.

Orwell's nightmare world is divided into three social classes, very much like Plato. At the top are the inner-circle Party members, who have all the power. Big Brother, whose likeness is omnipresent, is at their head, though it is never clear whether he is flesh and blood or a collective symbol. The next rank is the outer-circle Party members, abject functionaries whose lives are supervised by two-way TV screens. Below them come the Proles — the proletarians, who constitute the vast majority. Theoretically the revolution has been waged and won in their behalf, but in practice the government devotes remarkably little thought to their welfare. Since they are left alone in their animalian freedom and squalor, certain simple joys can come their way. They spend their mindless days as they will, singing the idiotic songs that are ground out for them by the songwriting machine, such as:

It was only an 'opeless fancy,
It passed like an Ipril dye,
But a look an' a word an' the dreams they stirred
They 'ave stolen my 'eart awye !

As I have previously intimated, the world of *Nineteen Eighty-Four*, at least on its upper levels, is not one of rollicking license. Marriage is strictly for procreation, or for 'making babies', as Winston's drab wife puts it. There is a flourishing Junior Anti-Sex League. Scientists are at work to find means of abolishing the organism, one research project that I had forgotten to mention. The rulers wish to build up as much sexual frustration as possible so that the suppressed energy can be sublimated into social desirable channels, such as adulation of Big Brother and good attendance at the mass hangings of 'war criminals' (*i.e.* prisoners of war).

The story of *Nineteen Eighty-Four* is similar to that of *We*. Winston, a member of the Party's outer circle, falls in love with a frankly sensual girl who takes a flippant view of leaders and ideology. In the glow of their romance he makes the mistake of saying disparaging things about Big Brother and the system. The two lovers are arrested and are separately subjected to a prolonged period of re-education by torture and psychological suggestion. The purpose is not merely to make them behave. This totalitarianism is really total. One heretic can make the whole body politic unclean. The Ministry of Love is a kind of secular inquisition, intent on preserving unblemished a holy society.

The main narrative follows the re-education of Winston. He proves moderately resistant. His main source of strength is a stubborn certainty that truth is truth, regardless of ideology; for instance, no decree of the Party can cause $2 + 2$ to equal 5. There are few passages in fiction more terrifying, more indicative of the ultimate, metaphysical degradation to which a man can be brought, than the scene in which Winston is finally trained to believe, *really* believe, that whatever the Party says is truth *is* truth. His salvation, and the cleansing of a threatened society, depends on his being wholeheartedly converted to collective solipsism. His instructor and tormentor, O'Brien, explains to him:

> "Only the disciplined mind can see reality, Winston. You believe that reality is something objective, external, existing in its own right. You also believe that the nature of reality is self-evident. When you delude yourself into thinking that you see something, you assume that everyone else sees the same thing as you. But I tell you, Winston, that reality is not external. Reality exists in the human mind, and nowhere else. Not in the individual mind, which can make mistakes, and in any case soon perishes: only in the mind of the Party, which is collective and immortal. Whatever the Party holds to be truth, *is* truth. It is impossible to see reality except by looking through the eyes of the Party. That is the fact that you have got to relearn, Winston. It needs an act of self-destruction, an effort of the will. You must humble yourself before you can become sane."

O'Brien then holds up his 'five fingers' and asks Winston to say how many there are. For a long time, despite repeated torture, he persists in giving the honest answer, 'four'. But eventually, thanks partly to torture and partly to the hypnotic power of suggestion, he sees a forest of fingers, impossible to count, and he accepts that he himself is unable to judge.

This is the beginning of his redemption. This is the final and complete abomination of desolation. There is little more to say about Winston. He becomes a beery, teary admirer of Big Brother. The fire that briefly burned between him and the girl is burned out and purged. He is a dutiful zombie, an un-man.

If one takes *Brave New World* and *Nineteen Eighty-Four* as archetypal dystopias, their points of resemblance are first worth noting. Each society is ruled by a small *élite*, which alone escapes the grosser kinds of psychological conditioning and brainwashing (I am forgetting about the Proles — they don't count, any more than the savages count in *Brave New World*). Each society has decided that social stability and freedom cannot be combined, and has opted for stability. Each makes careful use of applied psychology. But the differences are as striking as the similarities. The rulers of the Brave New World are compassionate happiness engineers, who genuinely desire the felicity of their subjects and labour scientifically towards this end. But happiness in the usual sense is no goal in *Nineteen Eighty-Four*. Or perhaps one should say that happiness has been redefined. Happiness is now the exercise of power for its own sweet sake. This kind of happiness cannot be generally distributed; the stamping boot requires a supply of prostrate faces. Thus there is a sadistic, diabolic quality to this world that is lacking in the Brave New World which, by contrast, has a kind of childish innocence, the joy of the little boy reaching into the ever-normal cookie jar.

As I mentioned earlier, Mr. Huxley has raised the question, in his *Brave New World Revisited*, of which nightmare is more likely to become reality. He argues that happiness-engineering is progressing rapidly and is more efficient in keeping order than the cruel methods employed in *Nineteen Eighty-Four*. Big Brother doesn't really need a torture chamber; the psychologists will supply him with gentle and loving methods to keep his subjects loyal — and happy. Mr. Huxley may be right. On the other hand, he does not sufficiently reckon with the positive satisfactions that power can give. Suppose Big Brother wishes not merely a stable society, but the pleasure of smashing an occasional human face beneath his hobnailed boot? In real life the Russian Revolution and the Nazi movement to an infinitely greater extent have demonstrated that this desire is a powerful one and can motivate men who are not inspired by pure revolutionary zeal.

With both novels, the reader ends by asking, "Could this system go on for ever?" There seems no way that the middle or lower orders could overthrow it. If any of them get rebellious ideas the methods of social control are highly prefected to suppress, by loving kindness or torture chamber, the slightest disorder. The only way either system could be overthrown is from the top. The ultra alphas in *Brave New World* could grow weary of the system and abolish it, or they might start quarrelling among themselves. The inner-circle of the Party in Orwell's nightmare could conceivably divide into factions and destroy each other, thus bringing about the liberation of chaos.

All this is scant comfort, but anyone reading these two novels seizes upon what comfort he can. Even the most dreadful society (whether it smiles idiotically or snarls) must still have a class of rulers who are something more than robots, who are able to think. There is always a chance that they will be assailed with immortal longings, wild dreams, and discontent — or private ambition — and will be moved to do unpredictable things, such as destroying the static perfection they have created. The only way the eternal survival of these two worlds could be assured would be to turn *all* their inhabitants into robots. Fortunately, robots cannot lead robots. A few men must be left. Another ray of light occasionally pierces the dystopian gloom. There are hints that even fairly ordinary people may have a stubborn core of individuality which can be eliminated only by physical death. David Karp's *One* (1953) is a grisly study of the brainwashing to which a college professor is subjected in order to destroy his sense of personality and superiority. His memory is destroyed; he is given a new name and new occupation. But soon a vague intuition of superiority wells up in him, and when he is summoned for another interview with the Authorities he is sure that his merits are about to be recognised. In short, he proves the despair of the system, and there is nothing left except to kill him.

CHAPTER NINE

Looking Backward at Dystopia

WE HAVE journeyed through some of the nine circles of hell, and gazed upon alternative horrors. What does it add up to?

The once-born, healthy-minded, and healthy man will say, "Nothing much." He will dismiss these nightmares as the neurotic self-expression of a small group of writers who, lack sturdiness of spirit. He may refer to 'failure of nerve' and brace his shoulders with extra confidence to meet the future he intends to create. He laughs with condescension when his friends turn to psycho-analysis, religion, tranquillisers, or all three.

The once-born, healthy-minded, healthy man — though he lives in the depths of Indiana — unknowingly joins hands with others overseas. The communist also is once-born, healthy-minded, and increasingly healthy. He agrees that the inverted utopias represent a failure of nerve, but he adds that this is not merely in the writers, but in the culture they sensitively represent. What has failed, says the communist, is capitalism. It is in its death throes. Deep down, Western man knows the game is up — capitalism has fulfilled its valid historical role, is now an anachronism, and is in its moment of agony, ripe for death but unwilling to die and let the new world be born.

It is true that one of the most ghastly dystopias has come from the U.S.S.R., but this is by an author who finally chose exile, and thus ceased to count. The nation's image of itself is the pink-cheeked peasant singing folksongs while driving a tractor on the collective farm, and the factory worker reading Marx, Lenin and Khrushchev after he goes home from setting new production norms. And in the new China, the blue-clad peasants learning the communal life or setting up blast furnaces in back yards hardly have leisure for the exquisite introspection and long, sad thoughts of the dystopians. As for the newly emerging nations of Africa and Asia, they are so preoccupied with the practical problems of food, education, sanitation and Cold War politics that they seem little inclined to cultivate imaginary nightmares.

You and I are inescapably children of the West, and as such we are denied the wholesome certainties of the communists. To every *yes* we say a *perhaps*. It is conceivable that the communists are right. Perhaps they are healthy primitives who have brought into the world a clarity of outlook, a simplicity of motivation, and a dynamism comparable to that of the early Christians who turned the weary Roman world upside down and transformed it into a new thing, with fresh vision and confidence. The Communists might succeed in something of this sort . . . for a few centuries at least.

But Western man, who is surely the inventor of footnotes, hastily adds that this may not be true at all. One must beware of analogical reasoning. There have been 'invincible waves of the future' to which the future did not belong. Hitler's Thousand Year Reich is the most recent example. Furthermore, it is not necessarily true that pessimism and self-doubt are signs of dissolution and failure of nerve. Anyone who reads Elizabethan literature is struck by its morbid preoccupation with man's littleness, decay, mortality — and yet the era was the beginning of England's greatest glory. It was in actual fact a time of heroic achievement, by men who often considered themselves the stunted descendents of the magnificent men who had preceded them. It seems that sometimes the mildly neurotic, who know that all men move through varying and elusive shadows and that terrors lurk by every path, are tougher than the well-adjusted cheerful men who laugh at them. If the communists do not sweep the world, if the globe remains divided more or less as it is for the next two or three generations, the test will come. Which camp, which manner of man, has the greater staying power in the teasing face of ambiguities, frustrations, uncertainties? Victory does not always lie with those whose cheeks are rosy and who read novels about tractor production instead of Joyce, Proust and Salinger.

But to return now to the Western world and its misgivings. I submit that the shift from utopian to dystopian fiction is important. Quite possibly, it foreshadows one of those really massive psychological shifts that sometimes occur over a whole culture.

Why has the utopian vision faded? I can think of two reasons. One is that utopia has failed. The other is that utopia has succeeded. Utopia has both failed and succeeded outside the bounds of the fictional page.

Not to play around with paradoxes, let me explain what I mean. When I say that utopia has failed, I mean simply that the 20th century has cruelly disappointed the expectations of the 19th century. When I say that utopia has succeeded, I mean that many things that seemed utopian a century ago have now come to pass — but the result is not utopian.

In my discussion of failure-through-failure and failure-through-success I shall not try to take the one, and then the other. It is more convenient to look at both types of failure simultaneously.

Let me point out first, however, that when our great-great-grandparents dreamed utopian dreams and committed them to paper or tried to implement them in real life, they operated on several tacit assumptions which we have already examined. One of the most important was the double faith in man's rationality and benevolence. Not that the Victorians were as naïve as they appear in our caricatures of them, but to be as hopeful as they often were they had to believe that humanity is rational enough, and altruistic enough, to be persuaded — in its own self-interest, if nothing else — to work together for a better society. Whatever was irrational or perverse in the human make-up could be eliminated or toned down by education, moral training, a juster order of things. The utopians influenced by evolution recognised the old ape who has left us the vestige of a tail, but they were convinced that man could partially direct the course of his own evolution, guiding it towards reason, kindness, peaceful co-operation.

Along with faith in man's reason and altruism often went a 'wave of the future' psychology. This was half a secularised version of a Judaeo-Christian concept — the meaningfulness of time and history — and half a derivative from the theory of evolution. It is true that the latter in its pure state is not teleological, and says nothing about 'better' or 'worse', but popular thought soon yoked evolution with Progress, making it goal-directed, and drawing from it the renewed hope of irresistible advances towards better things.

To sum it up, the 19th century easily believed in Progress, even inevitable progress. By Progress it meant a gradual advance towards self-evident goals: peace, social justice, diffusion of culture among the masses, democracy, the rights of the individual, plenty to eat, health, long life. Perhaps I am a belated survivor of an older era, but I confess that these utopian goals still sound good to me. One might wish to add others, but I am not impressed by the up-to-the-minute thinker who sneers at them, either in the name of God or science, and pronounces them superficial and naïve.

The 19th century had real reasons for believing in Progress, even inevitable Progress. Things were happening, mostly in desirable directions. Slavery was being abolished in one country after another, women were marching with banners and placards towards their rights, the scientist was busy in his laboratory, new medicines and new agricultural methods were improving the physical lot of mankind, industrial productivity was rising, literacy was bringing the Bible and *The Origin of Species* within the reach of the common man. There were rumours that some day the cat-o'-nine-tails and the noose would be put away in the museum. The great political movements were mostly in the direction of more democracy and greater rights for the individual. Most important of all, if one disregards the American Civil War (which, after all, had no catastrophic effects on Europe) there was no major war after Napoleon was banished to his private island.

True, the light beamed most brightly in the highly industrialised countries. The white man shouldered his burden among the dark skins and knew it would be centuries before the darkness lifted from their minds. But even for them, there was hope. In time, they would join the march of Progress — at the tail end, but still there.

Not to issue a catalogue of gloom, it is worth while to glance at the various components of the dream and see what has happened in the century that was supposed to be the fulfilment. Take slavery — it is true that slavery of a formal, open-and-above-board kind has almost disappeared, except in a few very dark corners of the world. But one becomes bogged down in semantics. Is it or is it not slavery when men and women are sent to labour camps for political reasons or no discernible reasons? Is it or is it not slavery, or at least involuntary servitude, when the masters of East Berlin erect a concrete wall and barbed-wire entanglements to keep their happy citizens from foolishly fleeing to the flesh-pots of the West?

Women have certainly made great progress towards their rights. In Israel a woman can march in the army with a rifle. Almost everywhere she can vote and enter the professions. I do not gainsay this progress, but I must point out that never, at least in America, has the relationship between the sexes been as confused as now; never were so many books written telling men how to be men and women how to be women. Perhaps, and I hope this is true, the present state of affairs is merely a transition and the two sexes will emerge from the psychological fog, each emphatically what it gloriously is, but each still more emphatically a human being. In other words, I rejoice in the rights that women have gained, but I argue that, as of the present moment, the balance sheet for both sexes is confusing. This is especially true of women, who are still so much under the shadow of men that their idea of 'success' is modelled on the other half; unconsciously they feel that to succeed they must be a man in a skirt, a thing as monstrous as a centaur. The 20th century has in large part 'liberated' women on schedule, but neither they nor the men from whom women were liberated yet know how to use their liberty.

The scientist is certainly busy in his laboratory; and a great many people would still be alive in Hiroshima and Nagasaki if he had taken an occasional vacation. One need not labour the point, so obvious now, that 'Science' in and of itself is neither good nor evil, neither utopian nor dystopian. It depends on who uses it for what. The scientist himself usually has little to say about the use. He is the kept-man of society. Society, or whoever bosses society, tells him what to do and decides how to use his discoveries. Atomic power can broil cities or electrify them.

But even the purely beneficent achievements of the laboratory, such as medicines that prolong life, are really double-faced. They help fill up the world with old people, often neurotic, impossible to please, lingering on unhappily and posing appalling problems to themselves, their kin and society. Meanwhile, the reduction in infant mortality sends the world population booming on such a curve that it is doubtful if increased food production will be able to keep pace for very long.

Literacy made every German capable of reading *Mein Kampf* but not of evaluating it; it guarantees that no American need be innocent of the comics nor of *Time*. It encourages the erection of billboards along all the most enchanting scenery in the United States. Literacy creates a public that can be quickly reached by slogans and ultra-simplified analyses of complicated questions. It encourages the cock-sure mind that remembers something read somewhere and knows it all. The unlettered peasant had his proverbial wisdom, half nonsense and half common sense or more. Beyond that, he knew that he knew little. But because the same twenty-six letters of the alphabet convey information to sage and tout-sheet reader alike, the illusion is encouraged that the ability to read is a kind of diploma guaranteeing knowledge and good judgement. Again, as with women's rights, I should not vote to turn the hands on the clock back. People have learned to read; let us work hard to persuade them to read something worth reading. Still, as of the present moment, it cannot be maintained with absolute assurance that near-universal literacy in the Western nations has achieved the gleaming goals that the Victorians set for it.

Not to paint too uniformly dark-grey a picture, let me

concede that any eclipse of the whipping post and the gallows is a clear gain, partly because it means less brutality in the treatment of criminals, still more because it deprives the public of degrading and brutalising joys.

I come now to the two greatest let-downs. The worldwide movement towards democracy and individual rights has been sharply set back in our century. The fascist movements were a frontal assault on the liberal and humane tradition of the West. Communism, as usual, is more ambiguous, and the final balance sheets are not yet in. One might grant — it can't be proved either way — that the present U.S.S.R. is closer to something that might be called democracy and individual rights than was Tsarist Russia. But again, semantics gets in the way. The Soviet use of the word 'democracy' corresponds to Western usage only in a Pickwickian sense, and thus what from the Western viewpoint appears as a depotism ameliorated by a little democracy (where harmless to the state) is from the Moscovite angle of vision a flowering of *true* democracy. At any rate, seen through Western eyes, which I do not apologise for possessing, the Russian experiment in democracy is so far blurred and dubious.

Along with this, the newly emerging nations have not rushed to set up functioning democracies complete with a full panoply of checks and balances and guarantees for the individual. These provisions often exist on paper, but the reality is most frequently a strong-man government; in many cases the man is getting stronger. The suspicion grows that democracy and individual freedoms are tender and specialised plants that blossom only in soil that has been fertilised by centuries of experience, including a continuing fertiliser of blood, sweat and tears.

War? The past knows nothing comparable to the two world wars. If there is a third, the two earlier ones will seem like innocent tribal conflicts with shields and spears.

Looking Backward at Dystopia

One other partial fulfilment and partial failure should be added. Utopian thought is one of the influences leading towards the welfare state. This latter is now a reality in Scandinavia and Great Britain, and is gradually taking shape in the United States, though our peculiar tabus cause us to call it by other names. I am for it, because we *are* our brother's keeper, and I want my brother to be mine. But the visible welfare state does not glow with the unearthly radiance of utopia. It's better than the old law of the jungle, but it is, shall we say, all too human, a thing as much of bureaucrats and the inevitable chisellers as of incarnate idealism. As usual, once you get some aspect of utopia, it begins to look shopworn.

What I have been saying all illustrates a double point. First, that the utopian vision has faded partly because various features of utopia have become real (literacy, women's rights, the welfare state, etc.), and there seems to be a built-in price tag on every utopian advance. In the second place, the utopian vision has faded because some aspects of utopia seem farther from realisation than a century ago (universal democracy, individual freedom, peace).

Perhaps it is premature to render even an interim verdict in a century such as ours, when the stakes are doubled and redoubled, for good or evil. One wishes to be one's grandchildren and see what will have happened. Perhaps also the utopian visionaries expected the impossible. They confused the Kingdom of God with temporal possibilities. They would be content only if middle-aged Englishmen and Americans strode around in god-like splendour, dressed in Greek tunics and sandals, with every banker reading Spinoza for recreation. For whatever reasons, disillusionment has set in, at least with many of the most perceptive writers. Some see mankind as sinking contentedly into a quagmire of soft sentimentality and sensuality, amused with cheap, cultural toys, content to be a well-treated animal rather than men. Others, such as Orwell and Zamiatin, have a darker vision of a mankind planning its way into hell on earth.

I have been talking about the actual events of this century and their impact on the utopian dream. I should now say something about one particular element of modern thought which on the whole has doused utopia with cold water. This is psychology. Of all centuries, certainly ours is the one most obsessed by the psychological way of thinking. If the average literate American has a frame of reference, a coherent pattern for thinking, it must be supplied mainly by analytic psychology, Freud in particular. I have found that I never have to teach my students the basic vocabulary of Freudianism. If they did not imbibe it with their mother's milk, it came with their pabulum. It is almost impossible to get them to debate any question with rational arguments *pro* and *con*. They convert each discussion into an exercise in lay analysis. They do not inquire whether Marx is right in his theory of economic determinism, but what factors of his childhood and psychological development led him to the idea. Psychology is also the gold-plated excuse-of-all-work. Where once a student who hadn't finished a term paper would be sternly told by his professor, "You are lazy" or "You are undisciplined", the culprit now tells the professor, as though this constituted a plenary indulgence, "I have a psychological block against writing this paper."

If pyschology in general — but Freud in particular* — is

* The behaviouristic school of psychology is more favourable to utopian thinking, and can undergird such an impressive work as Prof. Skinner's *Walden Two*. It is also a mainstay of the dystopias, which have exploited it with especial zeal. I think it is accurate, however, to say that Freud has had a more profound effect on the 'unspoken assumptions' of both the advanced thinkers and the man in the street than the behaviourists have had. The practical triumph of behaviourism is in selling cars and con ducting propaganda.

the modern frame of reference in which we live and move and have our being, it is relevant to note that Freud does not give a cheerful picture of human rationality and benevolence. The rational mind is a little patch of cultivated garden, surrounded by the cobra-filled jungle of the unconcious. The jungle is always threatening to overwhelm the garden; in your sleep you can hear the cobras hissing.

Civilisation to Freud is a fragile thing, never established once and for all, and to be maintained only at heavy price to the Id, which has to moderate its importunate demands. The price of civilisation is neurosis.

It is not my purpose to hold forth at length on psychology, nor am I competent to do so. But I must insist that the general assumptions of contemporary man, shaped as they are by analytic psychology, certainly emphasise impulse and blind desires, and minimise pure reason. This may be one of the main reasons for the decline of the utopian vision. If Freud is right, where shall we find our philosopher-kings?

Because it is so obvious, I shall simply mention in passing that many of the theological tendencies of recent decades are parallel to the matters I have been discussing. The optimism of the old social gospel was akin to the utopian mentality. Neo-Orthodoxy, with its dour emphasis on man's sinfulness, irrationality and finiteness, has many links with the frame of mind congenial to analytic psychology. In each case there is the recognition of the jungle surrounding the cultivated garden of goodness and reason; the jungle that never withers.

Let me now try to look at the waning of the utopian hope from another point of view. I shall begin by dogmatically stating that the two large-scale political attempts to create a tangible utopia are the United States of America and the Union of Socialist Soviet Republics. Take the first first. Note that the American system of government is based not on a gradual, 'organic' accretion of laws and customs, but on a constitution which was drafted at a definite time and place by a committee of philosophers, and thereupon ratified by the representatives of the people as a social contract. Of course, it reflects earlier customs and experiences and it is constantly modified by new amendments and interpretations, so that the Constitution today is in function a considerably different document from the one signed in Philadelphia. Grant all this — the contrast yet remains. England bumbled along through the centuries, beheading a king here and exiling one there, evolving parliamentary procedures, building up a body of Common Law like a coral atoll, and finally emerged with its present system of government, whose stability depends as much on a Public School accent as on any key document. America telescoped history by having a group of men sit down together, pool their experience and wisdom and write out a social contract.

That is the constitutional, the formal side of it. The informal side is harder to put into words, but it was a dream — call it utopian — a dream of mankind's second chance. American man was to be the new Adam, laughing at poisonous fruit, and happily creating a way of life free from the entrenched abuses and stupidities of the Old World. Disregarding the gloomy minority whose spiritual lineage goes back mostly to New England, Americans are Rousseauans by temperament. In their early days the great wilderness, apart from its inconvenient Indians, seemed a pristine world in which man could live cleanly and upright, and avoid the mistakes from which the colonists had fled to found a new country. The resolve, spoken or unspoken, was to devise a just world in which each man would have full scope for all his legitimate desires; a world in which the fulfilment of one mysteriously aided the fulfilment of all.

Looking Backward at Dystopia

If I may illustrate my point by an absurd remembrance from my childhood, I recall that I was a great amateur botanist, with a special ardour for trees. I lived near the Blue Ridge mountains, an area fabulously rich in deciduous trees. Half a pantheist, I felt a wordless *rapport* with all the native maples, oaks, tulip trees and the rest. There seemed a goodness and purity about them. But I resented the occasional Norway maple or other import planted in town. It seemed a weary and stained alien from a world that had lost its innocence. I did not know it, but I had the dream of the New Adam, living in the uncorrupted world of innocence. It was silly, of course. For the dream to be consistent, my white face needed to be replaced by a red one; my genes were an import from the world of the Old Adam. But it will illustrate the important point.

The New Adam has impressive achievements to his credit. The triumphs of productivity are unquestionable. So is the widely diffused high standard of living. A nationwide network of schools and colleges provides the greatest experiment in mass education ever undertaken. A more-or-less democratic form of government has been made to work. The vision is not a total failure. But how cheap and shoddy the tangible accomplishments are, when one compares them with the original dream. What exactly is the New Adam doing? Is he in a grey flannel suit learning to be an organisation man and coming home to his all-white child-centred suburb where the psycho-analysts prosper like shamans in a tribal village? Is he the farmer paid for not farming? Is he the worker who enjoys his job so much that he wants his hours cut down to thirty a week? Is he the artist whose paintings brilliantly evoke a private inferno — or is it a public inferno? Where now is the visionary gleam? Is the John Birch Society its custodian?

The dream is not dead but deadened. Meanwhile, America

grows older. There are graves with tombstones more than 350 years old. The New Adam has tasted various fruits, some of which are poison. Every year it is harder for him to keep a separate identity from the venerable Adam of older nations.

There was a time when mankind shared America's utopian vision of herself. The gates were open to all desiring to be reborn in innocence, and to share in the creation of new Eden. But Eden is subdivided now, the gates must be strictly guarded so that only a few come through. Meanwhile, what is the outer world to make of America? Is America seen as a country of chewing gum and Coca-Cola and TV and racial disturbances, or does it evoke a picture of universal education, the new symphony orchestras springing up everywhere, the most generous nation that has ever given a helping hand to weaker nations? Is it the sturdy farmer — there are still some — or the eunuch in the grey suit? It is all of these things. The foreigner sees America as a garish blur of confusing configurations; so does the observant American. The mysterious Oriental is matched by the mysterious American. The great American novel has not been written, for no one can grasp America as a whole. Here and there in the blur there is the authentic utopian gleam, and it is important. But all the while the electrical equipment manufacturers and their organisation men conspire to fix prices, labour racketeers prey on labour, public and business alike, and Mississippi strengthens its *apartheid*. TV sinks to new depths as civic orchestras rise to new heights. America is utopia, dystopia, and everything in between.

Disillusionment with America is grave enough, but the disillusionment with the Soviet Union is more soul-shattering. The American Revolution, after all, was a modest one. It was directed as much towards the recovery of the ancient rights of British-descended men as the creation of new rights. In many ways it was a conservative movement. But the Russian Revolution held the promise of the clean slate. It aimed not merely at new political institutions and rights, but at a radical and rational transformation of the economic and social structure of the nation. Marxism, as understood by the Russian communists, was not simply a political doctrine. It was to fulfil the purposes of economics, morality, religion, and aesthetics. It was a total way of life, the complete blueprint for the perfect society. Its ambitions were more grandiose than any Philadelphian dreams, and thus its failures and its ambiguous achievements are the more painful.

The Soviet Union has been the traumatic disappointment of our century. If you have read Arthur Koestler's novel, *Darkness at Noon*, you will recall the passage where the old Bolshevik is remembering the early days of the Revolution when every pronouncement of Lenin seemed like a revelation brought down from a new Sinai, and it was as though the human race were standing ready for transfiguration into a new species. To learn how deeply that dream gripped mankind, even those who never thought of applying for a Party card, you can do a bit of informal research. When you are with a highly intelligent and well-informed group of people in, or past, their late forties, ask them as tactfully as possible when they lost faith in the Russian Revolution. With some, the disillusionment came as early as the famine that Stalin deliberately created in the Ukraine. With others, it was the Moscow purge trials in the mid 1930's. The Spanish Civil War, in which the communists were as zealous to suppress the non-communist Left as to crush the official enemies, the fascists, was for many liberals the final fading of illusion. Others remained hopeful up to the Berlin–Moscow Pact on the eve of World War II. For still others, the destruction of

Warsaw which Russian troops could have prevented was the moment of truth. Some remained faithful to the dream and the gleam up to the *coup d'état* in Czechoslovakia, the Korean War, or the Hungarian uprising, or the Pasternak case. With some, a very few, the dream yet remains. The wistful faith lingers on, the substance of things hoped for and not seen, that in the U.S.S.R. there is a tide of events that somehow, despite all evidence, will carry men to a new and ideal order. The dream dies hard. It dies hardest in the hearts of those men who long ago lost their utopian hopes for America, and have only the Soviet Union left. If they lost this last hope, they might have to turn to despair or religion, alternatives equally distasteful.

Now the truth is that a great revolutionary movement can fail in its grand goals but succeed in lesser ones. The French Revolution did not permanently establish democracy anywhere, even in France, nor ensure the full rights of man, but it did close down a good many torture chambers and introduce a rational system of law in various countries. It also sowed good seeds of discontent that continue to sprout, so that the Bourbons of future times could never again have things all their own way. The Soviet Union, though not utopia, has many solid accomplishments to its credit. It has industrialised a backward country and by and large raised its standard of living; it has created a system of education that other nations must study; it has exerted a strong world influence towards racial equality and the break-up of the old colonial system; it has, by its competition, compelled many countries to re-examine their attitudes towards a multitude of social questions. In America it seems quite clear that the mocking voice of Russian propaganda has served to make us more sensitive to the status of the Negro, and more ready to take action.

It is important to recognise the real achievements of the

Soviet Union at the same time that we quite categorically assert, "This is not utopia," and add, though with a shade less dogmatism, "This is never going to be utopia."

I should sidetrack a moment at this point to clarify one point. Any well-informed Marxist would surely resent my applying the word utopian to the goals of the Soviet Union. Marx used 'utopian' as a pejorative term. He restricted it to the non-scientific socialists, whom he regarded as day-dreamers and impractical romantics. But I must insist on my use of the word. The Soviet Union *is* a utopian experiment. It has the classic elements: complete social blueprints drafted in advance, rational planning, a coherent philosophy behind all the plans. And whether or not a Marxist would apply the word utopia to the Soviet experiment, it is surely true that many Marxists and semi-Marxists have responded to the experiment as though it were about to bring into existence the land of heart's desire, which is simply another name for utopia.

The classical Marxist doctrines are pure utopia. The classless society, the withering away of the state, from each according to his ability and to each according to his need — what breathes more the spirit of utopia? The achievement of these goals could bring history to a stop; mankind would live happily for ever in the timeless perfection that so many of the utopias envisage for the human race as its final earthly goal.

Even many of the specific details of the Soviet experiment are commonplace to the utopian specialist. Plato posited long ago a three-class society, and the Soviet Union now has it: the *élite* of inner-circle Party members, the rank-and-file members, and the masses. And Plato, who advocated falsehoods to keep the masses contented, could not object to the Soviet propaganda with its big lies, medium-sized lies, vest-pocket lies.

From Utopia to Nightmare

Also, as Plato advocated, the Soviet Union had domesticated and utilised the arts for social ends. The result is, paradoxically, a kind of wholesome literature, representational painting and conventional music that the American business man, maddened on his cultural forays by tormented novels, crazy pictures and twelve-tone music, would find restful to his soul. Whatever the Party says is good art *is* good art, and at least in the recent past, whatever the Party says is good science *is* good science, as the Lysenke controversy illustrates. Thus the arts and to a large extent the sciences are made to dance to the utopian tune.

So much for the evidence that the Soviet Union is a venture in utopia-building. But leaving aside all quibbles over words, several things remain to be said. One is that, though the U.S.S.R. may not be utopia or the New Eden, neither is it a Brave New World nor the land of *Nineteen Eighty-Four*. It has not gone to a complete extreme in either direction, not even in the darkest days of its Iron Age under Stalin, whose name meant man of iron. And like all societies, it is a state of transition. One finds the frozen perfections and petrified nightmares only in works of literature. Because the final Soviet achievement is not available for display, ambiguities remain and hopes linger. Perhaps the Soviet Union of Stalin was a brutal period of transition, similar to the dark age of the spirit now enveloping China. Perhaps the course of social evolution will lead the U.S.S.R. simultaneously to more TV and bigger apartments and to less reliance on terror and lies. The growth of a large educated class and the gradual increase in foreign contacts should have a liberalising effect.

The unreconstructed liberal, who thinks he has said his farewells to the Russian dream, finds it returning to haunt him. Perhaps, he tells himself, the horrors of the Soviet system are only a necessary stage in an essential social

evolution. The character in *Darkness at Noon*, who insists
that one must flog the peasants to educate them to the point
where they will no longer consent to be flogged, may be
right. Other great liberations have demanded similar violence and cruelty. The freedom of the American Negroes
was purchased by Sherman's march through Georgia. The
liberties that Great Britain now enjoys were bought at the
price of a king's severed head and a considerable number of
people whipped, branded, or hanged, drawn and quartered
at various times. Great social changes do not come about in
the chaste atmosphere of high tea.

In such moods as these, the liberal speculates also on the
might-have-been's. In many ways, Russia was the worst
possible place for the great Communist experiment. It had
never had a Renaissance; it was still medieval in many ways,
slumbering under the Byzantine tsar, when the winds of
modernity at last tore through it and destroyed the old
fabric. Communism came to a country without a real tradition of individual freedom or prolonged practice in the art of
democratic self-government. How much of the tyrannical
and Machiavellian character of Soviet communism is due to
the inherent nature of the philosophy, and how much to the
Russian way of doing things? Perhaps Russia is not a fair
test case. Suppose communism had come first to England or
France or the United States. Things might have been very
different. Perhaps . . . perhaps . . . all history is filled with
perhaps.

At this instant, the liberal, whose state of mind is veering
swiftly back to the Popular Front psychology of the 1930's,
jerks himself up short and sternly announces to himself: At
least what concrete evidence we do have suggests that the
Soviet type of utopian planning demands too great a sup-
pression of freedom to be worth the price. Something less
sweeping, more moderate and gradual, but with greater

respect for liberty, is preferable. The American liberal thereupon renews his membership in the National Association for the Advancement of Coloured People, and Americans for Democratic Action, as his practical contribution towards gradualism. Meanwhile he is haunted by the fear that perhaps he is thin-skinned, and that history is really moving in its broad outlines towards the Soviet kind of utopianism.

I have spent more time on the Soviet Union than I intended, But this is significant. When utopia shows signs of breaking out of hard covers, men everywhere hold their breath to see what will happen. Once they did this with America and France; in our times it has been the turn of the Russians.

But let us forget historical fact for the moment, and return to fiction. Utopian fiction has waned; dystopian fiction has waxed. I think the inverted utopias are the mirror of the nightmares that obsess not merely a few writers but millions of men and women who are too inarticulate to put their fears into words. It was not by caprice that W. H. Auden entitled one of his books *The Age of Anxiety*, and that others have spoken of the Age of Tranquillisers, and that the most popular brand of religion is the peace-of-mind cult. A vague but insistent anxiety lurks barely beneath the surface of our minds. We try to localise it; to say that if the Russians would cease from troubling, or if we had job security or a happy sex life it would go away. But it is broader and deeper. There is the feeling that human destiny has slipped out of our hands. (Maybe it was never there in the first place, but once we thought it was.) Our very idealism and generous hopes and our careful planning may turn against us and make hell incarnate sooner than we think. We begin to feel like the proverbial men in an oarless boat, borne swiftly down a stream towards a waterfall whose roar fills our ears though we cannot yet see it.

Looking Backward at Dystopia

I would contend that the dystopias have an additional importance for the thoughtful student of society and history. The advantage possessed by the writer who deals with an imaginary society is that the stage is less cluttered up with permanent and apparently permanent fixtures. The ordinary realistic novelist must operate within the empirical facts of a particular time and place. The anti-utopian writer, like his brother the utopian, is free to present in stark essence his particular vision of the nature and destiny of man. He is like a laboratory technician, isolating various strains of bacteria, malevolent or benign, and observing them in a pure state. Thus the creator of imaginary societies can bring into focus either the ultimate dreams or the ultimate nightmares of the race, so that they can be magnified to clarity, studied, analysed, evaluated. Such a writer operates as social scientist and philosopher, rendering judgement on what is possible and what is impossible to man.

I submit in addition that many of the dystopian writers are the prophets of our times. I use the word prophet in something of its biblical sense, to mean one who observes society, evaluates it in accordance with principles he considers eternal, and offers messages of warning where he sees it going astray; messages not merely of warning but predictions of the wrath to come unless society renounces its false turnings. If Amos, Hosea, Isaiah or Jeremiah were alive, I think it probable that they would be writing and publishing inverted utopias. It is the prophetic form of our age. And for one person whose armour of self-deception is penetrated by pulpit preaching, there must be a dozen who have been pierced by *Nineteen Eighty-Four* or *Brave New World*.

CHAPTER TEN

Recurrent Themes

THE INVERTED utopia has become a standard literary. *genre*, and as such has acquired a stock-in-trade of devices and gimmicks. Many of them sometimes cluster in the same book, so that it seems an epitome of other dystopias, a sort of composite nightmare. For instance, L. P. Hartley's *Facial Justice* (1960) — a tale of the quest for equality carried to monstrous lengths — includes these familiar features: mankind has been almost destroyed by a third world war; much of humanity is still living underground; there is standardised clothing and even standardised plastic faces (the logical culmination of equalisation and depersonalisation); there is a dictator who is heard but not seen; a special class of inspectors constitutes the new *élite*; everyone is compelled to take a daily bromide to lower his vitality and level of restlessness; plastic trees and flowers replace the real things; numbers are increasingly serving for names; language is becoming simplified and standardised so as to discourage the thinking of odd thoughts.

The devices are means to an end, ways of poetically symbolising and dramatising certain insights into mankind's present or permanent condition. But a word of caution at this point — one can rarely single out a particular device and say that it is invariably dystopian. Most of them wear a double face. The plain clothing and standardised homes of one utopia will be the prison-like uniforms and plastic-surgery faces of a dystopia, in which the lack of ostentation has degenerated into a hideous levelling and cult of mediocrity.

Recurrent Themes

Let me illustrate this point by one of the most significant dystopian authors, Aldous Huxley. Belatedly he has turned utopian dreamer, in his novel *Island*. Apparently he has long been haunted by the horrors of his own Brave New World, and (as was already evident in his foreword to the later edition of the classic dystopia) has meditated upon ways in which mankind could not merely avoid the feelies and the worship of Our Ford, but could actually create a society better than anything ever seen on earth. *Island* is therefore Huxley's vision of what a human society might conceivably be, if men used their brains and good will to create it.

Now the intriguing thing about *Island* is that it is in so many ways *Brave New World* still. In the earlier book, people take doses of *soma* to have beautiful dreams; in *Island* they consume the *moksha*-medicine (a mushroom derivative) to achieve cosmic consciousness. Both *topias* involve sexual mores that are casual, but in *Brave New World* sex is for fun, and in *Island* it is both for fun and for heightened consciousness. In each imagined world there are forms of psychological conditioning; in the earlier work, these are used to make robots of people, and in the recent novel the aim is to moderate their more dangerous impulses and to aid them towards self-understanding and the mystical vision. In short, similar devices have been used for very different ends. The question is teleological. *Brave New World* aims at stability and flat-spirited happiness; *Island* is a basically Buddhist country, though much aware of modern science and its possibilities, and its goal is that of the 'Higher Utilitarianism, in which the Greatest Happiness principle would be secondary to the Final End principle' ('the unitive knowledge of the immanent Tao or Logos').

If utopia is social planning that produces good results, dystopia is most often social planning that backfires and slides into nightmare, whatever its original intent may have

137

been. With this distinction in mind, it is time now to look at some of the recurrent dystopian devices and themes and see whether they have any relevance to practical life. To some extent, I shall have to ask you to take what I say on faith, since I shall be deriving part of my evidence from books I have not had time to summarise. But I can assure you that if you develop a taste for dystopias — and the thing is habit-forming — you will quickly enough discover that all the themes I shall mention are so standardised you can predict with considerable confidence the presence of a couple of them in any work of this genre.

One other thing I should say in advance. I am startled to find how often the recurrent themes have rather a biblical ring. That is part of what I meant when I spoke about the 'prophetic' role of the dystopian writers, but I now have in mind something broader than the strict prophetic tradition. I am thinking of the total way that the Bible looks at the human scene, and the parallels between specific biblical insights and what the anti-utopians are asserting. The resemblances can rarely be attributed to the overt piety of the authors. They are a mixed lot, but probably a majority are not Christians in any definable sense of the word. The historian might simply say that biblical concepts have so permeated our culture that no writer, be he atheist, Judeo-Christian believer or California Zen, can entirely escape them; they are 'internalised'. There is some truth in that. But there is still more to it. Perhaps there really are some immutable truths about man and society, about his possibilities and limitations; perhaps the ancient writers of the Bible discovered certain of them, and the dystopians are rediscovering them by dint of hard thought and close observation. Boston is the same city, whether you drive down from Vermont or fly from Chicago. I shall try not to overstate the resemblances, and I know that one must bear always in mind that biblical writers viewed the world in theocratic terms alien to most dystopians. But where there seems a valid parallel, I shall point it out.

Now for the recurrent themes, which I shall enumerate at the cost of some unavoidable repetition of observations made earlier. One of the most frequent comes as something of a surprise. This is the disparagement of the physical universe, nature and the human body. Somehow one would expect to find that a nightmarish society is gross and sensual, that it goes in for a Nature cult and perhaps a sort of pantheism. But though traces of these attitudes can be found by diligent search, the general picture is quite different. The dystopian world is likely to be finicky, fussy, squeamish, even puritanical in its own way. It is prone to down-grade the body and to fence out untamed nature.

This hostility towards nature has a utopian background. The trim garden rather than the untidy wilderness is the utopian ideal. Often there is a suggestion that nature must be domesticated. H. G. Wells would get rid of most animals, except the cute ones. The typical utopia is a city surrounded by well-tended farmland. This urban bias of utopia becomes exaggerated in dystopia. In C. S. Lewis's *That Hideous Strength*, a leader of the demonically-inspired Institute of Co-ordinated Experiments looks forward to the day when all trees, messy and ugly things that they are, will be replaced by artificial ones, more beautiful than the original and cleaner. It is noteworthy how many imaginary, dystopian cities are surrounded by high walls to keep the wildness out. The assumption seems to be — and perhaps it is valid — that a thoroughly planned society is so definitely a human artifact that plastics and structural steel are more 'natural' than the chaotic and teeming life of nature. Nature must therefore be exterminated, tamed, or confined to special reserves.

From Utopia to Nightmare

Rarely in either utopia or dystopia do you get a sense of awe and reverence towards the miracle of the created universe. What you have is man's imperious mind, lording it over nature. Nature is a *thing*, to be exploited or destroyed. The proud mind claims and exercises a more than biblical dominion over all natural things, by forgetting that nature, too, is a creature of the same creator and entitled to its humble but inalienable rights.

The dystopian distaste for the body is still more striking than its cold disdain for nature. In *Nineteen Eighty-Four* we have the Junior Anti-Sex League and scientific experiments to abolish the orgasm, so that frustrated sexual energy can be diverted towards more spiritual ends, such as love for Big Brother and the special hate periods. In *The Machine Stops* and *Star of the Unborn* the white, flabby bodies shun even a handshake. Bernard Wolfe's *Limbo*, which I shall shortly discuss in another connection, has a special class of spiritual heroes who undergo amputation of arms and legs so that their wicked limbs can do harm to no man.

It is profoundly unbiblical, this hostility to the body. Granted, here and there one finds segments of Christianity with a hang-dog attitude about the body and its functions, but this is a perversion of the central Christian tradition, and cannot be remotely justified by any balanced study of the Bible. The Scriptures exult in the juicy fact of the natural world, and the solid reality of the human body. Both are viewed as the creation of a God who delights in making milk and honey available, and who has chosen to combine the continuation of the race with the most exquisite of physical pleasures. To be more ascetic than God, unless there is some special reason for the renunciation, is to follow not the Scriptures but the Platonic dialogues. The body can be a snare and a temptation, but the answer is to sacramentalise it, by using it in accordance with God's purposes, rather than scorning it or trying to by-pass it.

In its central tradition Christianity has always insisted that the worst sins, such as pride and envy, are spiritual. They can wreak more hell on earth than any constellation of carnal sins. To this insight, the inverted utopias offer confirmation. The society of *Nineteen Eighty-Four* is not a nightmare because men eat too much or indulge in illicit sex, but because their minds and spirits have become corrupted until they call black white. In their collective solipsism they have tried to become as gods, controlling reality itself by an act of the will.

One final thought on this subject. 'Spirit' as such is neither good nor bad. Satan remains a spirit, but a fallen one. He is probably free of the vices against which the prudes inveigh: it is doubtful whether he smokes, drinks or fornicates. To Satan the whole sacramental system of Christianity, the Incarnation and the doctrine of the resurrection of the body would seem revoltingly vulgar. The sight of a proud, ascetic man excites Satan more than any motley crowd of drunks or fornicators. He knows he has a better beachhead for action.

So much for the anti-nature bias in dystopia. Another of the truths recognised in many dystopias is that man is in danger of losing his wholeness and his sense of personal identity. The latter loss is sometimes symbolised, as in *We*, by the substitution of numbers for names, as though a person were nothing but a statistical fact. In milder form it is suggested by the uniforms that the inhabitants of dystopia often wear.

Wholeness is most easily destroyed when a person's life is divided into watertight compartments. We can see foreshadowings of this in real-life today. Many a man is one man at church, another at the dining-room table, a third when he concludes a business deal. Every time he 'changes his hat' he becomes a new being; he is not sure which of his *personae* is the real *he*, if a real *he* exists. Perhaps he is nothing but a cluster of functions. In the anti-utopias this tendency is often carried much farther. Sex and family life afford particularly good opportunities to put asunder what God has joined together. For example — when we are thinking normally we look at love, marriage, sex, parenthood, and child-rearing as one package. In the anti-utopias the package is frequently broken up into three or four separate fragments. Sex may become simply a harmless pastime, a release for tension, or a ritualistic act of solidarity with the community and its deity. Or it can be de-glamourised and restricted to the sober (and preferably joyless) purpose of procreation. In any event, romantic love is pretty sure to fall by the wayside and be replaced by casual lust — or nothing. Marriage is sometimes permitted in dystopia, though choice of mate is often in the hands of the state. Often, too, breeding is completely outside of marriage. Aldous Huxley merely went one or two dystopian steps farther when he invented the hatcheries. In *Brave New World* the 'package' is logically divided into its separate component parts. Sex is for fun or religious devotions, procreation is via hatcheries, love and the family and motherhood are useless components of the package and have been discarded.

Even in those inverted utopias that keep some semblance of a traditional family system, the children are likely to belong to the community and be brought up not as sons and daughters but as citizens, remembering their childhood public nursery as home. Marriage, though still permitted, is drained of half its content.

All this has a close bearing on the sense of personal identity. Psychoanalysts today are kept busy helping people find some content in the pronoun 'I'. In the assorted nightmares of tomorrow their task would be triply difficult, because the individual is broken down into his separate roles and functions and there is little communication between I_1, I_2, and I_n. This all rarely happens by accident. It is the deliberate planning of the rulers. By weakening the sense of individual identity, they make it more likely that the average man will merge his own frail identity with the social whole and cease to demand that he be called by a name instead of a number.

Inverted utopias also bear witness — and somehow it comes as a surprise in the context — that man is incurably religious. In *Brave New World* the inhabitants invoke Our Ford or Our Freud, make the sign of T, and partake of strawberry *soma* Communion. Huxley's later nightmare, *Ape and Essence* (1948) shows the brutish survivors of atomic war as worshippers of Belial. They offer human sacrifices and make the sign of the horns. Perhaps, however, this book does not really belong here, since the Belial devotees do not make utopian pretensions. More central to the dystopian tradition is an idolatrous adoration of society, the life force, evolution, or the deified leader. The normal religion seems to be worship of Big Brother or the Well-Doer, who is the embodiment of the community. Opposition to him, or even a lukewarm attitude, is not simple crime but sacrilege.

Outright atheism seems almost as rare in dystopia as in real life. If one thinks of religion as the ultimate concern, most men have it. The American who does not worship an authentic God is almost certain to have a substitute deity: The American Way of Life, Free Enterprise, the Standard of Living, the arts — or sex — at least something. Whatever his deity, he offers sacrifices to it, whether he is the young executive conforming to the expectations of his superiors or the young artist half starving in the service of his Muse.

From Utopia to Nightmare

It is permissible to point out another biblical parallel here. The Bible devotes remarkably little time to the menace of atheism. The biblical viewpoint seems to be that atheism is a rare and puny adversary compared to idolatry. And the Bible hints that gods have consequences. A man's religion (even if he doesn't call it that) will shape his character and his deeds. A nation's religion (even if not so labelled, as in the case of Soviet communism) will shape *its* character and deeds. The Bible does not agree with the common, tolerant American assumption that religion, any religion, is automatically good. President Eisenhower was not paraphrasing Scripture when he said, "Our government makes no sense unless it is founded in a deeply felt religious faith — and I don't care what it is."* The Bible intolerantly insists that the only good religion is true religion, and that false religions — such as the idolatry of ancient times — are more the stratagems of Satan than parallel roads to the truth. In the dystopias one often feels that the society's implicit religion — such as the worship of Big Brother in *Nineteen Eighty-Four* — is the worst thing about it, and that an authentic atheistic movement would be a first step towards simple decency and sanity.

One need hardly dwell on the depersonalisation that prevails in the inverted utopias. This is closely linked to the point I made earlier — that man is manœuvred into losing his wholeness and sense of identity. Men and women become numbers, interchangeable parts in the functioning of society. They have no inalienable right to lock a door or pull a shade down. Their very right to live is not a right but a privilege, based on their continuing ability to serve a society which is all-in-all. The result is a ghastly parody of the Christian virtues of love and humility. People transcend themselves by

* Quoted in Peter L. Berger, *The Noise of Solemn Assemblies*, Doubleday & Company, Inc., Garden City, N.Y., 1961, p. 63.

dying to self and being reborn as cells in the social body. But it is a trivial death and a trivial rebirth.

In the inverted utopia the individual's self is not redeemed but engulfed. He literally loses himself in the larger whole. This is what sets this kind of 'death' and 'rebirth' apart from the classical Christian concept. Christianity indeed holds that the self must be surrendered to God, but He doesn't hang on to it, nor does He absorb, amoeba-like, the self into His own being. He is not a cannibal. Rather, he cleanses the surrendered self, imparts new life to it, returns it to the owner. The Christian saints in their fantastic and picturesque variety of personality and temperament are the farthest possible remove from the emptied 'numbers' who are the interchangeable parts of the dystopian machine.

What I have just said leads on to a point that at first seems outrageous — that too much unselfishness can be a bad thing. In one anti-utopia after another we find people emptying themselves of individual longings for the sake of society as a whole, and the paradoxical result is that no one is happy, no one is fulfilled. 'Society' as an abstraction may function in beatific bliss, but its component numbers go about heavy-hearted or so void of private life that they are incapable of either happiness or misery. If the individual members of a dystopia are not wretched or stupefied and dull, they may alternatively achieve a kind of pseudo-fulfil-ment, a blasphemous caricature of the mystic's unitive vision — a fulfilment that moves the person away from his essential humanity but not towards God. He advances to-wards absorption in the social whole, which is worse and cheaper than the sum of its parts.

From the viewpoint of Christian humanism — and I suppose that is how I would label my angle of vision — the trouble is that the individual who submerges himself in society is giving himself to himself. The multiplication of numbers is not the introduction of a new dimension. Indeed, society is often less subtle, less perceptive than the individuals who compose it. Many a participant in a lynching bee is a decent chap as long as he does not assembly with more than half a dozen of his fellows. The Christian has to conceive of self-surrender in terms of an additional dimension, God.

This somewhat discursive discussion leads us back to the question of the body. We have seen how dystopia is suspicious of it and its inbuilt urges; the pseudo-angel is commended more than the lusty animal. This is not accidental. A man's sense of individuality and identity is mightily aided by the stubborn mechanisms of his own body. When he is hungry, *he* is hungry, not the social whole. When he wants sex, it is not that society *en masse* is in a mood for mating. The very possession of a body that can tread on rough ground and bump against obstructions is a reassurance, a proof to all except the philosophical idealists and solipsists that there is something real about me, something crudely tangible that gives me the right to say 'I'.

One of the most common ways in which an inhabitant of dystopia discovers the spirit of rebellion in himself and sets out to express it is through falling in love, or at least in lust. D–503 in *We* was a happy member of the social hive until he met I–330. His physical love led him step by step into rebellion against the sacred state. Winston, in *Nineteen Eighty-Four*, did not really question the divinity of Big Brother until physical passion (not much romantic tenderness) assailed him. He was aware that every instance of copulation was an act of revolt against the system. "You like doing this?" he asks Julia. "I don't mean simply me: I mean the thing in itself?" She replies, "I adore it." The book continues:

146

That was above all what he wanted to hear. Not merely the love of one person but the animal instinct, the simple undifferentiated desire that was the force that would tear the Party to pieces. . . . Their embrace has been a battle, the climax a victory. It was a blow struck against the Party. It was a political act.

The dystopian world has a great deal of internal logic. For example, if the individual citizen finds the entire meaning of his life in subordination to the social whole, he has no particular reason for staying alive when he is too old or ill to do his job. In many anti-utopias, it is true, he can retire from work fairly early, but he has been so conditioned to be a cell in the social body that one imagines him at loose ends, with little inner life, regardless of his state of health. So, logically, euthanasia is one of the recurrent themes — as indeed it also is in the straight utopia. In both kinds of *topia*, elaborate facilities are often maintained for those who find life stale and useless.

On the purely human level, it is hard to quarrel with this. A man's life belongs to himself and still more to society. If he and his society wish to end it, who is there left to interrupt with a dispute over ownership?*

* The euthanasia theme is found also in some utopias that have a strong religious colouring. More mentions its merits, and C. S. Lewis, in *Out of the Silent Planet*, has the *hnau* undergoing euthanasia at a certain fixed age. This is done by the spiritual overlord of the planet, Oyarsa, and represents not so much a relief from old age as a transition to a different state of being.

CHAPTER ELEVEN

Recurrent Themes, Concluded

I COME now to a common dystopian theme that interests me particularly. If it represents a valid insight into the human condition it points to a built-in limiting factor in all schemes for total social perfection. This is that you can't have it both ways. You can have a society aquiver with creativity — arts, sciences, technological breakthroughs, everything — or you can have a safe and stable society. You can't choose both. The reason is that creativity and destructiveness are both parts of man's restlessness and imagination; they are two sides of the same coin. If you get rid of one, you get rid of the other. Thus a highly creative society, such as Periclean Athens or Elizabethan England, is certain to be filled with social turmoil — discontent, plots, rebellions, fanaticism. An extremely stable society may indeed carry on the creative traditions of the past — as China under the later emperors continued to produce exquisite pottery and verse — but the wilder flights of creativity will not be found.

The truth of this is for better historians to debate; but I think there is a good deal of empirical evidence for it. At any rate, the dystopian authors time after time assume its truth. Their imaginary societies have stability, but literature and the arts are reduced to trivialities, mainly propaganda, and the sciences are kept under strict control and permitted only such socially desirable activities as the perfection of brainwashing.

Dystopian ingenuity has devised a varied array of methods

148

to dampen discontent — and creativity. In Anthony Boucher's *Barrier,* where the state's duty is the maintenance of the 'Stasis of Cosmos', even changes of time or key in music are strictly prohibited. Every variety of indoctrination and brainwashing can be found in one inverted utopia or another — hypnopaedia, Doublethink, Newspeak, elaborate civic rituals to engulf the individual in a collective consciousness. Sometime the brain is prenatally stunted to make it tractable, or everyone (as in L.P. Hartley's *Facial Justice*) is compelled to drink a daily draught of bromide.

Several anti-utopias employ a particularly telling symbol, physical mutilation: the prefrontal lobotomy. In *We* it becomes a routine rite of passage. All 'fancy', all restlessness is surgically excised. The entire population becomes happily obedient to the Well-Doer, and thinks no more turbulent thoughts.

Bernard Wolfe's *Limbo* (1952) also uses the lobotomy idea. The earlier part of the book is set in an unknown island in the Indian Ocean where a primitive people, weary of wars and private conflicts, has developed a crude lobotomy to take the violence out of their more unmanageable citizens. An American surgeon, escaping from the next World War, happens to land there. Finding that the surgical mortality rate is high, he lends a helping hand by performing the lobotomies himself. But he soon sees that aggressiveness is inextricably linked with creativity and responsiveness. Native artists who undergo the operation lose their drive; women are frequently unable to experience orgasm afterwards. The beneficiaries of the lobotomy become contented, low-toned, lazy, harmless.

After the surgeon returns to America — a great atomic war has intervened — he finds that the most morally and spiritually sensitive people are undergoing voluntary amputation of their limbs, so as to make war physically impossible.

The same thing is happening in Russia. But since their minds are unchanged, they find a way of constructing mechanical limbs, better than the original, and soon a desperate race develops between America and Russia to corner the supplies of a very rare mineral, columbium, which is essential in the manufacture of synthetic arms and legs. This leads to war. The moral is neatly dramatised. Man is not dangerous because he has teeth that can bite and hands that can hold a rifle or press a guided-missile button. He is dangerous because of his mind and spirit. The only absolute cure is something equivalent to a lobotomy. But the cure deprives us of future Homers, Michelangelos and Einsteins, as well as of Genghis Khans, Hitlers and Bluebeards.

This notion of mutilation has a bearing on a biblical tale, the fall of man. It has often been remarked that Adam and Eve fell upward as well as downward. The downward fall was the loss of innocence, the revolt against God. But they fell upward into first-hand knowledge of good and evil, creativity and destruction. They were banished from paradise into a world, our world, where many things that had been theoretical possibilities were to be tasted as realities. Thus a new meaning came into all goodness and creativity, for they knew also the tang of the opposite.

To recognise these truths — dystopian and biblical — is to bring us to a realisation that the ability to choose good or evil, creativity or destructiveness, is grounded in man's radical freedom. Remove one, remove the other, A lobotomy might have kept Hitler a contented house painter. But it would have kept Einstein away from the special and general theories of relativity.

There is no exit. What can be done is simply what the great moral and religious teachers have always tried to do: train the half-savage beast so that he will want to channel his ambiguous restlessness into harmless or even constructive channels. It is conceivable that space exploration may become the moral equivalent of both war and armed robbery. The businessman grown rich by destroying his rivals and despoiling the public can sometimes be led to philanthropy and find himself putting his ill-gotten gains — perfectly valid coin of the realm — into schools and hospitals, or subsidies for young writers who will compose novels dissecting and denouncing his kind. A climate of public opinion can be created that will encourage creativity and benevolence, and discourage destructiveness and aggression. I for one should like to see more than lifesize statues of Dr. Salk and Robert Frost erected at prominent intersections in that monumental city, Washington, while they are yet in the flesh; and it would help if a few national holidays commemorated the deeds of scientists, artists, and social workers, rather than the weary procession of warriors and politicians.

Next comes another important theme which I venture to call the 'Law of Reverse Effect'. By this I mean that if you try too hard for something, or try for it at the disregard of other and equally valid goals, you are likely to get the opposite of what you want. Many of the anti-utopian novels deals with societies in which material abundance has been fanatically sought and shabby poverty achieved. In others, the original quest for freedom and justice has produced tyranny and injustice. You will recall Evelyn Waugh's story, *Love Among the Ruins,* in which people are so kind to criminals that the sum-total of kindness in society is diminished rather than increased. In all these cases a goal, desirable in itself, has been inordinately pursued.

The Machine Stops pictures a society that has tried to take care of every eventuality by a marvellous machine which not merely does the work but makes most of the decisions. The experiment is a success until the machine breaks down. Then the Law of Reverse Effect takes its revenge. The people are less competent to survive than if they had never invented the machine in the first place.

A particularly brilliant and convincing study of the Law of Reverse Effect — though he doesn't use the term — is provided by Michael Young in *The Rise of the Meritocracy 1870–2033: The New Élite of Our Social Revolution* (1958). This perfectly plausible book describes what happens in England when the nation discovers its productivity is slipping in comparison with that of other countries. The cause is found in entrenched privilege, the educational system in particular, which is based more on hereditary privilege than ability. Two great social transformations shift the emphasis to capability. One is a reform of education, with much testing and measuring, so that the brightest young people get the best education and rise swiftly to the top of the social and economic ladder. The other is the replacement of the old seniority system in industry with promotion by merit. The effect of these two reforms is to give almost perfect equality of opportunity, and incidentally to put England in the vanguard of industrial progress, now that its best brains are used where they will count the most.

Everything is subordinated to the goal of letting merit have free scope. What counts is I.Q., for it is I.Q. that is needed to keep the economy booming. For a time it looks like utopia. The old class lines break down. A boy (or girl) from the poorest family can rise to the top simply by demonstrating his intelligence. The son of a baron may find his education cut short and his career directed into some humble occupation. The dream of Plato — and of Thomas Jefferson — is fulfilled. Merit creates its own natural status.

But the Law of Reverse Effect strikes back. The old class system, though unjust, had been tolerable because everyone knew it was absurd. The privileged classes themselves admitted that many an aristocrat wearing the wig of a judge was a bumbling incompetent, less capable than the person who brought him the mail. This realisation imparted some twinges of humility to the privileged classes and kept the under-privileged from feeling that their objective social status was an automatic measure of their deserts. The new system changes all that. Merit is now automatically rewarded. The men who rise to the top really *are* superior. Those who remain at the bottom, or sink to the bottom, are genuinely inferior.

Finally, it is noticed that in actual practice the children of intelligent parents are usually intelligent. More and more, the future *élite* is drawn from *élite* families. This is not because they have any inside track, but simply for genetic reasons. Most of the good genes are now concentrated in the new upper class. At this point the right wing of the Conservative Party proposes that the hereditary principle be restored. It is obvious that nearly all the brains are concentrated in the *élite*. Why should their children be bothered with all the testing and measuring? This proposal touches off disorders and a counter-movement — to get rid of the educational system with its emphasis on pure I.Q., and create a new type of common school in which less testing and measuring goes on, and more attention is given to the intangibles of personality — kindness, responsiveness — that are not immediately useful in industry. The discontent is particularly strong among women. In theory, they can rise to the top, but since most of them are married the competition is really unequal, and they feel that the qualities they excel in, such as compassion and depth of personal relationship, are unfairly devalued by the emphasis on I.Q. alone. At the end of the book, it looks as though the revolt may succeed.

One could not ask for a neater illustration of the Law of Reverse Effect. First, a society with the best intentions in the world aims at abolishing privilege and class distinctions by letting merit forge ahead. The result is that the old ascendancy of birth is replaced by the ascendancy of brains, a dominance much more bitter to endure. And to complete the irony, it seems that a new hereditary class system evolves, more galling than the old one. The rebels are really saying that the desire to give free rein to I.Q. was inordinate. Society has tried too hard for too narrow a goal. It has been punished by evolving a worse social stratification than the one it set out to destroy. To put total emphasis on I.Q. is as absurd, as inordinate, as to put it solely on brawn. A man is more than brains, he is more than brawn. If there is to be a ranking of men, additional qualities must be taken into account.

I do not wish to rival Parkinson in the discovery of new 'laws', but I must say I think the Law of Reverse Effect has an importance that transcends the covers of dystopian novels. I can give one or two examples. The late but not lamented Senator McCarthy had appeal for people who wanted to be sure, absolutely sure, that America's national safety was not threatened by an enemy within. They went looking everywhere for communists, crypto-communists, fellow travellers, pinkos and bleeding hearts. The results of the hunt was twofold. They managed to silence a good many people not even faintly communist — the kind of men and women who might otherwise have worked most effectively to initiate the changes and reforms needed to give American society the necessary vitality to withstand the communist challenges and to improve its standing in the uncommitted nations. Thus the McCarthyites laboured mightily towards a stagnant society, incapable of reacting with dynamic new approaches to new situations. They helped prepare the way for the sterile drift of the Eisenhower years.

Recurrent Themes, Concluded

But that was not the sum of their accomplishments. They had a baleful effect on some liberals who had pretty well given up their old Popular Front dreams of the 1930's. I had the chance to see how each new blast from the Junior Senator or his adorers tempted the old liberals to fall back into the psychology of long ago. Since McCarthy was such a Neanderthal, and since he set himself up as the hero on the white horse to battle with the communist dragon, that dragon began to look a shade less uncouth. After all, his main lair was a quarter of the globe away, and McCarthy's was in Washington. I don't want to overemphasise the point. In the bosom of some elderly or middle-aged liberals the illusions of the Popular Front period had an Indian summer, that is all. Certain liberals began facing a situation that did not seem altogether hypothetical — if they had to choose between the mindless Know-Nothing-ism of the McCarthyites or the highly intellectual if partially misguided rationality of the communists — which would be the lesser of the two evils? Fortunately, McCarthyism waned, and I doubt if permanent damage was done to many liberals. But it is certain at least that McCarthy did absolutely nothing to increase their determination to stand up against the communists.

Let me now take another example from real life — from the liberal side. I am thinking of race relations and school integration in particular.

Since I have some lingering traces of a Virginia pronunciation, let me first say that I rejoice in the Supreme Court decision of 1954. Having thus established my credentials as a liberal, I can go on to say that even the laudable goal of school integration — and beyond that, I hope, the crumbling of all racial barriers — can be inordinately pursued. It is one thing to state, and I believe the Supreme Court did, that no child living in a school district can be kept out of that school solely because of colour. It is quite another thing to insist that a child has an inalienable right to go to a school where both blacks and whites are represented. I am thinking of situations in metropolitan centres of the north where great racial ghettoes exist, and practically all the inhabitants within a given school district may be of one race. One can argue, and it has been argued, that the schools should be used as an instrument of social change; that pupils should be taken in buses to distant schools so that each race will have a chance, at least during school hours, to rub shoulders with other races. I grant that some understanding might come of this. But so might a kind of schizophrenia. The children return at evening to their ghettoes. Meanwhile, the local school as a community focus is weakened. A school is much more than a place where children, anybody's children, are educated. It is best a place where the children of people you know are educated, and where you meet with their parents for a variety of community purposes. A diminished community spirit will mean less zeal for maintaining good schools, and less zeal for other things that need to be done, such as a frontal assault on the ghetto system itself. If the schools suffer and community morale suffers, the last state of the under-privileged races can be worse than the first.

I may be wrong. I hope I am. Perhaps the schools are the one instrument through which society can pull itself up by the boot-strap. But I doubt that the schools can do it alone. If they are expected to, watch for the Law of Reverse Effect. After all, the heart of the racial problem in the north is not schools but ghettoes. If the ghettoes can be opened up in both directions, and if the *apartheid* of the suburbs can be cracked, this will accomplish much more than any number of school buses taking bewildered children to remote schools where they are interesting laboratory exhibits. Once the ghettoes are gone, and once *apartheid* crumbles along the elm-shaded streets of suburbia, school integration will automatically take place.

Such are two examples of the Law of Reverse Effect. It throws a rather penetrating light on many of our concerns, and the practical moral is that, in pursuing one laudable goal, you must be sure that you are not becoming so fanatical in your methods, and so neglectful of other legitimate goals, that the thing will kick back, producing conditions worse than those you are trying to remedy. In short, the 'Law' demonstrates that the cardinal virtue of Prudence is relevant to public affairs.

Dystopians are often right, too, about something that is closely related to the Law of Reverse Effect: the familiar observation that Ends and Means cannot be divorced. The inverted utopias register a demurrer to the character in *Darkness at Noon* who wishes to whip the peasant so that he will finally refuse to be whipped. The more probable upshot, says the dystopian, is that the whipper will grow to like the job and will be unwilling to resign it, even though the peasant may begin to fight back. The whipper will think of fancier and fancier reasons why flagellation is good for the individual and society; he may evolve a whole metaphysic in justification. By some such logical system as Doublethink he will prove that 'A lash is a kiss,' and will brainwash the peasant until he craves constant kisses. The original reason from strong-arm methods will gradually be forgotten; cruelty will cease to be a means and will become a continuing end in itself.

In both *We* and *Nineteen Eighty-Four* the apparatus of the police state was presumably considered at first a necessary evil for a transition period. But the transition has hardened into a permanent pattern. There is no longer the pretence that some day, however far in the future, the spies and hidden microphones and torture chambers can be done away with. As instruments of a sacred revolution they have become sacred.

This is no new truth. Sensitive men of goodwill have always been aware of it. It is a fact that could, put into practice and carried to its logical extreme, paralyse all action. Criminals could not be jailed, babies could not be spanked. Morally sensitive men are at this moment desperately divided over the clearest dramatisation of the dilemma: What about nuclear weapons? Those who favour unilateral disarmament argue quite simply, as does Bertrand Russell, that it is both better and more moral to be Red than dead. Equally sensitive men on the other side contend, as their first line of defence, that if you have enough bombs you may not have to use them; secondly, that even if it came to nu-clear war and the widespread devastation of mankind and its works, this might be preferable to a globe dominated not necessarily by the Russians but perhaps soon by the Chinese communists in their iron age of self-righteous brutality, or by some people who in turn would build bombs, overcome the Chinese, and be still worse; thirdly, that the purpose of human life is not simply to be alive, but to have a life worth living, and that it is preferable to run some risk of total extinction of the species rather than to resign oneself to an indefinite future in which the least scrupulous nations will shape all mankind into whatever hideous image they choose.

The same dilemma was faced during the Hitler period. Perhaps it was most acute for the conscientious Christian. Though Christ once wielded a whip in the Temple, his life was otherwise singularly free of violence on his part, and a Christian cannot by a torturing of the texts make him into the prototype of the happy warrior. The Christian pacifist obeyed the gospel by refraining from dropping blockbusters on the Germans. By refraining, he made it possible for the Germans to continue shoving the Jews into gas chambers. He acted with love towards the Germans. His love for the Jews was less evident. He failed to use the only methods that could have stopped the genocide. The non-pacifist dropped bombs; this hardly amounted to an act of love towards the Germans. Pacifist and non-pacifist were both caught. By what they did or did not do (and the two are morally equivalent) they added their share of evil to the world.

I have stated and illustrated the dilemma not in order to settle but to clarify it. We move through a grey world in which purity of means plays into the hands of monsters, and ruthless means may turn us into monsters. I think Prof. Joseph Fletcher is right in his insistence that the Christian must always operate on the principle of 'love-*cum*-calculation'. He should try to maximise love, and do as little evil as possible in the process. But the 'calculation' is the catch. It involves the study and evaluation of circumstances that are always too complex to be mastered fully; it includes a shrewd guess as to the probable outcome of a given course of action, and all guesses are dubious. Neither pacifism nor non-pacifism can be elevated to the status of eternal principle. At one juncture of history a Christian may find reason to be a pacifist, at another he may discover that the ancient doctrine of the 'just war' is not always sub-Christian.

I have been giving extreme examples, suggested by the extreme weapon. But the same dilemma exists in the quietest moments of ordinary life. Take the case, a real one sometimes, of the professor who is intolerant of all views except his own, and who bases grades on agreement with his ideas. Perhaps a student, who hopes to get into graduate school and become a social worker, is taking the course. It is some controversial subject like philosophy or political science. On the final examination there is an essay question. 'State and justify your viewpoint on . . . . . .' The student needs at least a B to keep his average up and get admitted to graduate school. Shall he put his tongue in his cheek and express the views the professor wants to hear? What harm will it do? Isn't it really the professor's fault? And wouldn't the student be doing real harm to society if he courted a C or D and weakened his chances of becoming a trained social worker? As I outline these arguments, I find myself drawn to the student's side. And yet . . . How many times can one argue this way without creating a permanent cast of mind? The student writes a dishonest examination. He finds that in another course — a required one — he can scrape through by a little outright cheating (after all, he is hurting no one; he will never pretend to be a mathematician). With a third professor he puts on an *ad hoc* personality, pretending an avid interest in the English madrigal in order to coax a good letter of recommendation. In graduate school and beyond will he find that 'playing it safe' has become a fixed habit? When he becomes a social worker will he be one of those wretched men who can always discover good pretexts for going along 'with the system' for the sake of good goals that are less precise after each dubious decision?

Everyday life and the sombre warnings of the inverted utopias both point towards several morals. One is that bad means should be employed as sparingly as possible. The burden of proving their necessity is always on the individual who uses them. He ought to be more than 50 per cent sure, on the basis of all the facts he can gather, that the results are likely to be mostly good. The other moral is that the uneasy conscience is a priceless boon. It should not be put to sleep by any process of reasoning or conditioning. To revert to our original examples, the pacifist and the non-pacifist alike should remain aware that they move amid shades of grey, and that no decision is going to be an act of love towards everyone. The conscience should remain uneasy; it need not be neurotic. A Christian, at least, can recognise his inescapable guilt, and then offer it to God as much as he offers any achievements to Him, and receive back forgiveness and love. The real human monsters are those who for good reasons become so accustomed to evil means that they invest their means with the sanctity of their ends and never wake up in a cold sweat at night.

The next thing I want to talk about is something that is more implied than stated in dystopian literature. It is this: the universe is what it is, the moral order is what it is, human beings are what they are. There are limits to how much any of the three can be reshaped. If handled too callously, the three will strike back.

This does not mean that man has no scope for manœuvre. From the biblical viewpoint, he has been handed a Do-it-yourself kit in the form of the earth. It is filled with half-completed jobs and abundant materials. He is given dominion over it. But dominion implies a loving and intelligent master. He has scope to turn forests into farms — but not if the land is so steep that rains will quickly wash away the topsoil.

He can also refine and adapt his moral codes to meet changing conditions, but if he gets too far from the essential moral platitudes — part of the very structure of reality — he will be struck down. The dystopias suggest that a completely new moral code, such as one that flatly reverses the Golden Rule and its many non-Christian equivalents, would be so savage an assault on the universe's moral structure that Morality itself would take reprisals, perhaps by reducing the society to idiocy or demonism. The point is that it is one thing to change marriage laws so as to take account of the new status of women and the decline of the patriarchal family. It is another thing altogether to get rid of marriage. It is one thing to be kind to criminals in the hope of rehabilitating them; it is another to make national heroes out of them.

Similarly, the inverted utopias imply that there are limits to the malleability of man's nature. Certainly, within very broad limits, he can be trained to be warlike or peaceful, contemplative or activistic — but the limits still exist. For instance, as we have seen earlier, if he tries to become as the angels, his weakened body will be at last his undoing, if he has not first been destroyed by the pretentions of his arrogant mind.*

Man's room for manœuvre is great. But not all things are possible. The physical universe, the moral structure of reality and man's own nature are all limiting factors. Just *where* the limits lie cannot be known in advance. Perhaps science will find a way of building extra-sensory organs into all men. Our descendants may create a full atmosphere on Mars and colonise it. A time may come, as in *Erewhon*, when illness will be considered more reprehensible than crime, and one can conceive of situations in which this attitude would not offend against the moral structure of the universe. The limits are not drawn on a chart. All that the dystopias imply is that limits are there.

* The continuing debate over whether such a thing as 'human nature' actually exists, or whether it is a social artifact, is discussed with great insight in a remarkable article, 'Life, Liberty and the Pursuit of Welfare', by Joseph Wood Krutch (*The Saturday Evening Post*, July 15, 1961). Mr. Krutch cites some experimental evidence which bridges the two viewpoints. It seems to be true that 'man is malleable', and can be conditioned into almost any personality and outlook. But, the authors points out, it is much easier to instil some attitudes than others. It seems to be 'natural' for the child to grasp such ideas as a real right and a real wrong, justice, moral responsibility. The contrary ideas are much harder to implant. Thus it is possible to continue speaking of 'human nature', in the sense that man takes readily to some ideas and with reluctance to others.

They imply also that the important thing is the attitude of men as they push towards the limits. They can explore and exploit and manipulate as though the physical universe, moral reality and human nature were so many raw materials. Or they can explore in a spirit of reverence. Reverence means that the farmer cutting down trees to extend his fields has a sense of awe for the miracle of topsoil and vegetation; he will not act hastily until he is sure the results will be good. He behaves towards the universe with love-*cum*-calculation. Similarly, a philosopher or utopian planner wishing to reform the family system is disqualified unless he begins with a sense of awe at what the family, with all its imperfections, has already accomplished. He must be in love with it, if he is lovingly to modify it.

In *The Abolition of Man*, C. S. Lewis states there are two ways a writer can use the language he has inherited. He can regard it as mere raw material, to be reshaped according to his will. He may carve and recombine it into some lifeless abomination like Basic English or Newspeak. Alternatively, he can look with reverence but no false shyness at the language that Chaucer, Milton, Auden and nameless merchants, lovers, peasants and adventurers have bequeathed to him. Lovingly, tenderly, aware always of the language's own integrity and unique flavour, he can work within it, creating new words where needed, recharging old words with new meanings, even evolving new syntactic patterns. I should personally say he could go as far as Joyce and still be within his linguistic inheritance. It is the attitude that is crucial: either he is working from the inside or he is imposing his will from the outside.

The dystopian recognition that there are built-in limits to how much we can change the physical universe, the moral order and our nature, adds up to a kind of natural piety which can exist apart from any belief in God. The trouble with the dystopian citizens is that they lack wonder and awe. They are all set to twist and remodel and recombine everything in accordance with abstract blueprints. It is the story of the mind and will grow great to the point of malignancy. In Greek terms, it is *hubris*. If *hubris* comes, can Nemesis be far behind?

The final recurrent theme that I shall discuss is one with obvious biblical parallels. I shall even borrow my term from the Scriptures: the 'saving remnant'. This is found in utopia and dystopia alike. Plato's philosopher-rulers and H. G. Wells's samurai are a creative minority, deliberately evolved, to provide the drive and guidance for society. Many utopias provide for a similar *élite*. In a utopia the creative minority is the vanguard of society, its point of heightened consciousness. In the inverted utopia, the creative minority or saving remnant is the rebels against a nightmare, who are trying to change it from within to something better — or if that is impossible they are ready to leave and create a saner world elsewhere. In either case, the real hopes of humanity rests with this minority rather than with the larger society and its horrors.

This theme is sometimes developed in fantastic form. In *The Space Merchants*, by Frederik Pohl and C. M. Kornbluth, the world is run by advertising agencies whose sales pitches constantly pursue the unhappy consumer. A saving remnant of 'Consies' (conservationists) flee by spaceship to Venus, where the sight and sound of the commercial will no longer trouble. In that most remarkable science fiction novel, *A Canticle for Leibowitz*, the Roman Catholic Church and its monastic orders are the saving remnant during a new dark age, and when civilisation and atomic war returns, it is a spaceship filled with bishops, priests and religious that carried the hopes of the earth to a distant planet where a small colony has already been established. If our globe is burned bare of life, the human venture will continue, complete with a new papacy if need be on the other planet.

In *Brave New World* the saving remnant is ironically represented only by a few futilely discontented Alphas and the pitiful figure of Mr. Savage, too primitive to have any lasting impact on the perfect world he briefly enters. The theme is developed more systematically in Huxley's *Ape and Essence*, where the morally and spiritually perceptive flee to a co-operative community and laboriously lay the foundations of a rational civilisation that may some day spread after the sons of Belial have destroyed themselves by their own bestiality.

C. S. Lewis's *That Hideous Strength* shows the almost-successful attempt of the N.I.C.E. to take over England. The universities are manipulated, the popular press sings the praises of the brave new venture in the social application of science. The opposition consists of hardly more than a manor house of seemingly ineffective people, mostly Christians, who are not deceived. By their perseverence and sheer staying power they hold the line until powers partly magical and supernatural can bring about the downfall of the N.I.C.E.

I have already mentioned the role of the creative minority in *The Machine Stops* and *We*. Ayn Rand makes particular use of the theme, as the creative men and women in her books quietly depart from stagnant worlds and establish new societies.

The Bible was composed by men ignorant of Gallup Polls and electronic computers. It assumes that God is no respecter of statistics. The inverted utopias concur. Sometimes the seemingly futile man who has bowed the knee neither to Baal nor to Big Brother has the future in his stubborn hands.

CHAPTER TWELVE

Dystopian Demurrers

I HAVE taken you on a guided tour, highly selective, of dystopia, and have pointed out some of the recurrent themes. I should like now to backtrack. Earlier I mentioned nine assumptions, many of which at least are likely to be held by any utopian dreamer. Let me now list them again and indicate what the dystopian would say in reply.

1. *Man is basically good.* The dystopian says No. He doesn't deny that there is goodness in man, but he says it isn't strong and constant enough to be depended on too far. Even the most elaborate system of education, character training and conditioning will not make goodness a reliable trait in either the masses or the *élite*. Man is and will remain a mixture. The savage and the sadist and the plain schemer and the importunate ego are always lurking within him, sometimes hidden from sight, but ready to spring.

2. *Man is exceedingly plastic.* Here the dystopian comes closer to agreeing. He is impressed by the advances of practical psychology and brainwashing. Man can be moulded so that his heart beats faster at the likeness of Big Brother, so that a sexual orgy becomes his communion with God and the Social Whole. He can be trained to go through the motions of subordinating his selfish interests to those of society. He is a clever dog; he can be taught a great repertoire of tricks. But when man is radically reshaped it is at a price. He acquires, perhaps, a pseudo-altruism, a pseudo-goodness. He is like a person in a hypnotic trance, obeying the hypnotist. Those who are thoroughly conditioned and

brainwashed are something less than real human beings henceforth; they are more akin to the wretches who have submitted to an actual lobotomy. If real goodness and altruism are to exist, rather than the benign motions of puppets, men must be left free to choose between good and evil. The dystopian might also add or imply that, though the newborn child is something of a *tabula rasa*, some messages can be written on the blank slate more easily than others.*

3. *There is no need to set up a dichtomy between the happiness of the individual and that of society.* The dystopian says this is true in heaven, but not here. When men submerge themselves in the social whole they are engulfed in a magnification and multiplication of self. Society is man writ large, sometimes the worst of man. Also, the goals of society have to be of a broad and impersonal kind: survival, maintenance of order, etc. Society as such is little concerned with immortal longings, delicate raptures, obscure agonies. Society regulates mating and marriage; society does not fall in love with this girl or that. Society is by its nature more coarse-grained than many of its members. The individual who seeks his fulfilment by being a bee in the hive must give up the nuances of his nature. He may be rewarded by a kind of secular beatific vision as he 'dies to self', but it is a false fulfilment, not good for him, not good for society. The dystopian also asserts that too much emphasis on the well-being of society can lead to a world in which the collective whole is flourishing but not a single one of the automata inhabiting it is capable of happiness.

4. *Man is a rational being, and can become more so. His powers of reason can be harnessed to the task of creating a society that makes better sense than any existing society. There is nothing sacred about the social institutions that have so haphazardly*

* See page 162.

evolved. Just as real science has supplanted a great mass of half-scientific, half-superstitious folklore, so a real science of society can create something much better than the accidental society now existing.

To take these points up one by one, the dystopian says two things about reason. First, that man is intermittently and partially a rational animal, and secondly, that reason itself must not be equated with the benevolent will. The devils may have a purer power of reason than we do, but you would not engage them to build your utopia. Reason, like science, is two-edged. And even reason submitted to goodwill is subject to self-deception, rationalisation, and the myriad tricks by which we find good reasons for our special biases and interests.

About the further clause, the dystopian does not deny that existing societies have grown like Topsy, though he might insist that many apparently absurd customs and attitudes reflect an age-long process of trial and error, and serve a real but obscure purpose. He would say that planners who wish to start with a clean slate don't reckon with the complexities. Actual societies, as the anthropologists have taught us, have an internal logic. Can a society be created from scratch and have a sufficient internal logic? Isn't it better to work from within the existing societies, lovingly and cautiously making changes where it seems they are needed?

There is an analogy. When the calorie was first discovered as a unit of energy, it seemed sensible to devise prison diets that would guarantee an adequate number of calories per day. With a clear conscience, society fed its criminals on calories. But the prisoners began to get scurvy and other afflictions. The trouble was not that they had too few calories but that no one yet knew about vitamins. The dystopian would be inclined to say that any society, in an intuitive or trial-and-error way, discovers the social vitamins needed for its well-being, and that a utopian planner, dreaming grand thoughts, is likely to construct a society strong in calories but weak in vitamins.

Public housing projects in both Britain and America often demonstrate the same knowledge of calories and ignorance of vitamins. The planner forgets, for example, that young married couples have parents and sometimes like to have them living less than an hour's journey away in another project. Or the planner is so intent on 'cleaning up the streets' that he makes them dull; the result is that few of the local people choose to stroll around of an evening, and hoodlums can come in and have the streets to themselves. Many old-style slums have a better morale and sense of neighbourliness than communities that spring complete from the planning board. This does not mean that public housing is bad, but that the planner needs to deal with more than the 'calories' of life.

5. *The future holds a finite number of possibilities, which can be sufficiently foreseen for practical purposes.* The dystopian says No. Outrageous novelties may upset the most careful plans. The insect you import to get rid of some other bug may eat up your garden. The Law of Reverse Effect may turn the planner's work upside down. The dystopian is more inclined to bumble along, feeling his way and hedging his bets, rather than assuming that he can feed all the relevant facts into a computer and thereby anticipate the multiple consequences of every decision and act.

6. *The purpose of utopias is man's earthly welfare.* Utopians and dystopians alike differ greatly in their attention to any transcendant goal, such as salvation or heaven. In general, they are both more concerned with having a tolerable order of things here on earth. One world at a time, if there is more than one world. So the disagreement is over methods. The utopian would create earthly beatitude by rational planning;

the dystopian wants to make sure that the planning doesn't engender worse evils than it cures.

7. *People don't get tired of happiness.* Utopias have a way of depicting their inhabitants in a state of sustained contentment, if happiness is too strong a word. They go about their pleasant and useful tasks, conscious that they are serving the social whole. Little is usually said about private satisfactions or personal griefs. Dystopia emphasises the perverseness of men, their restlessness, their ability to grow weary of a flat and virtuous contentment. Perhaps the utopian has a 'classical' cast of mind, and would like to see the world a formal garden of well-laid-out paths and proper statues available to public gaze. The dystopian is more of a 'romanticist', and considerably more of a psychologist. He knows that man is obsessed with finitude, time and death, and that a little neurosis is part of our heritage. He is not so sure that the bland happiness of utopia is enough. If he had to chose, he might opt for more agony and more ecstasy.

8. *Rulers can be found who will rule justly, or men can be picked and trained so that they will rule justly.* The dystopian agrees with Lord Acton's famous *mot* — the more power a man has, the greater the danger of corruption. In a utopia, where the rulers are convinced that they are the selfless servants of the public good, the danger of corruption would be heightened. Power is habit-forming; too much of it in anyone's hands is an invitation to danger. The dystopian would argue that the American Constitution, with its fussy system of checks and balances, is a practical recognition of this important fact.

9. *Utopia is not opposed to freedom. It will lead to 'true freedom', as individual men and women find their own destiny fulfilled by co-operating freely with the purposes of society.* This is closely related to point 3, and the dystopian would make a similar rejoinder. Please define 'true freedom', he requests.

He seems to recall that the nazis and communists alike have been fond of the phrase. Does 'true freedom' really mean a flowering of the individual as part of the social whole, or does it merely signify that he has been so brainwashed he is incapable of thinking any thoughts or having any longings of his own? In that event, the dystopian would settle for plain freedom. He knows what *that* means.

CHAPTER THIRTEEN

The Bourbon and the Jacobin

I REACH this point with a guilty conscience. I don't think I've been fair to utopia. It is time now to permit a utopian counter-attack. There is more to the utopian tradition than one would think from reading a succession of dystopias. Despite anything I may have said I am convinced that if the utopian dream dies, something profoundly human and perhaps profoundly Christian dies with it.

Let me borrow the language of the French Revolution and suggest that in social and political thinking there are two eternal types, the Bourbon and Jacobin. For my purposes, these terms must be divested of any implication of 'right-wing' or 'left-wing'.

By Bourbon I mean simply the person who has a deep-felt sense of the complexity and rootedness of any society, and is extremely reluctant to change anything in it, for fear that the delicate plant will be mortally injured. He is likely to be strong on intuition, weak on critical analysis. He prefers the evils that he himself recognises to the unknown evils that may ensue if the organism is tampered with. He is willing to tolerate a multitude of apparent absurdities, even though he cannot say what purpose they serve. He senses, in a way he can seldom articulate, that they are part of the total organism as it has evolved, and though he cannot prove that they have any use, this does not prove the contrary. Their very existence and persistence is to him strong evidence that they may not be useless in reality. Perhaps their usefulness is not in themselves, but as part of a total pattern of relationships. For example, just to speculate — the British love of fox-hunting is not a way of bringing dinner home; it does not prepare young men for the conditions of modern war; it is no better for physical conditioning than a good set of tennis. But the British Bourbon would oppose the animal lovers with what seems an immoderate zeal. In the cloudy but sometimes profound depths of his mind he senses that fox-hunting just possibly is a key element in national survival. Perhaps the pursuit of the fox is a ritual act which renews a *rapport* with nature and of man with man; it may be essential training to develop *esprit de corps* and loyalty in future diplomats; it may be as vital a part of the national *mystique* as the bull-fight seems to be in Spain.

The Bourbon mind is maddening to the Jacobin, for it seems from the outside like nothing so much as the absence of mind. The Bourbon appears to sprinkle holy water over things as they are and call them blessed. He can be found defending with his intuitions and entrenched power such obvious evils, in various parts of the world, as whips, nooses, *apartheid*, the right of the aged to die for lack of medical care. In the realm of the arts, he is always busy praising the art forms that his grandfather detested. The Bourbon, as I use the term, can even be a communist. There is evidence that Soviet communism is settling into a new orthodoxy and tradition, and that the entrenched bureaucrats are the new Bourbons, stubbornly protecting the system that was created by the generation just before them.

In defence of the Bourbon, whether he be of the left or right, it must be granted that he was there before the anthropological research teams arrived. He knew all along that society is not a machine but an organism, with an internal logic; that its various features fit together in a weird and wonderful way — and that the surgeon who wishes to remove one part or graft another into the social body had better be sure he knows what he is doing. The Bourbon would probably add that the science of social anatomy and physiology is still in such a primitive state that no social surgeon is competent to do much more than remove a few splinters from the social hide, or take out a set of obviously diseased tonsils. Beyond that, it is best to do nothing. After all, the body functions.

By implication I have already defined the Jacobin. As I use the word — I must emphasise this point again — it has nothing to do with 'left' or 'right'. The Jacobin is simply the great theoriser, the planner, the apostle of the *tabula rasa*. He wonders why one should tinker in trivial ways with society. Why not sit down, take a long look at the social scene, meditate on first principles, and draw up new blueprints? These do not have to be completely different from the existing society. There may be much in society that is good and can be incorporated without radical change into the future design. After all, a new owner remodelling a house may keep the charming living-room as it is, while enlarging the kitchen, and incorporating part of the upstairs hall into a bedroom. But if parts of society are retained, it is because they happen to conform to some specification in the abstract blueprint on the drawing board.

The spirit that moves the Jacobin is 'Why?' He demands that each feature of the social organism present its rational credentials. Indeed, he is reluctant to use the word organism. To him society is rather an organisation, based ultimately on the social contract. He is at ease with written constitutions and formal rules and regulations, for these can be rationally debated, amended and even supplanted. He is bewildered and irritated by the vague but exceedingly persistent network of subtle attitudes, habits, customs, ways of doing things. When the Bourbon of the right or left launches into a quasi-mystical defence of blood sports, debtors'

174

prisons, primogeniture, compulsory Latin and Greek, male dominance — or the eternal rightness of Soviet realism in the arts — his reaction is to say contemptuously, "You don't know why you believe in these things — you are rationalising your habits and conditioned reflexes."

The two types are always with us and have always been. Sometimes it is difficult to classify a given person. That interesting political figure, Senator Goldwater, comes to mind. Offhand, one would put him in the Bourbon column. He passionately wishes to preserve whatever elements of rugged individualism and *laissez-faire* capitalism still flourish in America. But since the actual America of the 1960's is a semi-welfare state, one might argue that Senator Goldwater is actually a Jacobin of the right. He has a precise and doctrinaire social blueprint in his mind. If it were politically feasible he would like not to stabilise the present situation but systematically to roll it back until it more closely approximated the good old days. In his dedication to a *theory*, a blueprint, and his willingness to subordinate the complex and subtle realities of 20th-century America to the blueprint, he reveals the impatient drive of the Jacobin.

At any rate, the distinction should now be clear. The Bourbon, as I use the term, wants to keep things pretty much as they happen to be. The Jacobin wants to remake society to fit a blueprint.

In these terms, the utopian thinker is obviously the Jacobin. For the last time, I emphasise that this implies neither 'left' nor 'right'. There are many socialist utopias, but there are also utopias that no philosopher of the Manchester school could criticise. The utopian is a Jacobin simply because he deals in broad theories and is convinced that one should rationally decide what a good society is and then create it.

The dystopian is the Bourbon. This does not mean that in

his private life he may not be a reformer and a crusader for this and that. But in his dystopian writing, he is concerned to show that the imposition of abstract social designs on the living human material does not always work out the way the laboratory tests have predicted. He wants us to be aware of how strange, wonderful, delicate and perverse any society is, and how impossible it is for the dreamer and schemer to create, *ex novo*, a society that will not develop grave kinks and hitches. He has a more modest view of the scope of reason than the utopian. He is not sure that any human mind, or a committee of the best minds, can encompass all that needs to be known about man. He is pretty sure that a society springing straight off the drafting board will be shallow, superficial, more a clanking construction than a living thing. And he knows in his intuitive bones that the best laid plans can be, and probably will be, frustrated or preverted by the flesh-and-blood men who must carry them out.*

The essence of the mainstream utopian tradition is planning. That is what links Plato, More, Bellamy, H. G. Wells, even H. L. Hunt. That, not any particular social or economic theories. This being so, the utopian at this point makes a valid observation. What is so strange about planning? he demands. The so-called organic society, which the Bourbons extol, is much more an artifact, a deliberately created thing, than its admirers are wont to admit. This can be easily seen in America with her carefully drafted constitution. But England as we know her is also a nation that came into being through successive acts of planning. Definite decisions, embodied in laws, broke the ties of England

---

* Sometimes a writer is a dystopian towards other men's utopias, but a utopian when it comes to his own blueprints. Aldous Huxley does not object to *all* planning. He has his own vision of utopia, embodied in his recent novel, *Island*.

with the Roman Church and created a new pattern of church-state relationships. Other laws whittled the House of Lords down and magnified the House of Commons. In our century it has been laws (another name for planning) that have converted England into a welfare state. Oxford and Cambridge themselves were the result of deliberate planning; they did not rise from the ground because dreamy-eyed medieval scholars happened to converge on the scene, each carrying a building stone. Every society contains a large element of quite conscious planning. It is the ivy that gradually grows over the works of man which creates the illusion that here is an organism, not an artifact.

To all this the Bourbon replies that what begins as 'artifact' may end as part of an organism; and that in any case there is a total spirit to a society and such subtle inter-relations as to forbid doctrinaire attempts at over-all re-modelling or the substitution of a completely new model. Muddling along is the height of wisdom. Feel your way, trust your intuitions especially when you can't justify them, know in your bones as well as in your mind that whatever you do is in keeping with the deepest needs *and feelings* of society.

I can now come to a series of conclusions that will not be startling in any way.

In the history of human thought, the utopian is primary, the dystopian is secondary. The utopian is like the artist, the dystopian is the art critic. The utopian's proper job is to dream dreams and prod the imagination and conscience of mankind. The dystopian's job is to take a long look at the dreams, handle them, look for defects, try to imagine everything that could go wrong. This is a secondary job, critical rather that creative. But it is important and in some times and places it can be crucial.

The jibes of the dystopian are not the signal for us to

abandon utopia but to dream more intelligently and profoundly. We must plan with a loving and precise knowledge of existing societies and their apparent irrationalities. We must take into account the subtleties of spirit, tone, emotional satisfactions. We are called upon to know our sociology, anthropology and psychology as well as philosophy, political science and economics. But we must not stop dreaming. We must not stop planning.

It is easy now to see why the 20th century has been a time when utopian dreams shone less brightly. The essence of utopia is planning. In the 19th century, when America and western Europe made such a fetish of 'freedom' that it was virtuous to leave a man free to starve and his children free to work in the coalmines, planning seemed the cure for the sicknesses of society. The 20th century has its craw full of planning. The nazi movement was thoroughly planned. Communism is planned. The organisation man lives a life planned for him. In Washington, no matter who inhabits the White House, planners stoke the electronic computers and the planning continues day and night.

It has been discovered that planning can produce drab, sometimes wicked results. Even good plans can somehow lead to less than the gleaming goals that inspired them. And each act of planning doubles and redoubles the stakes. If planning turns sour, it can produce evil on a scale that would have been impossible in a looser world. Thus it is that many intellectuals have been driven to what I call the Bourbon point of view. They are so fearful that planning may get out of hand that they say with Berdyaev: "peut-être un siècle nouveau commence-t-il, un siècle où les intellectuels et la classe cultivée rêveront aux moyens d'éviter les utopies et de retourner à une société non utopique, *moins* '*parfaite*' *et plus libre*."

And yet, it won't do. The utopian impulse — rational

planning — has augmented freedom as well as limited it. Planning took away from the coalmine owners the freedom to employ small children, but the same planning gave the children freedom to play in the fields or even go to school. It was planning that took away from the workman the freedom to carry home his entire pay-cheque, but the same planning gave him the freedom to have some dignity in his old age, rather than being thrown back on the mercy of his children or the workhouse. If the utopian impulse, the rational dream of justice on the planning board and on the march, can produce results such as these, it is hard for one in Christian conscience to join the Bourbon or dystopian camp entirely.

Yet there *is* a diversity of gifts. The Christian who takes seriously his role as a social and political being may conceivably find his vocation as a Bourbon. In that case, he becomes the critic of every attempt to do larger-scale tampering with the social organism. He asks constantly, "Will it work? Have you taken all the factors into account?" He points out complex details that the impatient Jacobin has overlooked. He urges that grand experiments be tried out on a small scale before society is irrevocably committed to them. But if the Christian is going to be a Bourbon, let us hope he will be a genuine one, aware of the rich confusion and dense texture of his actual society, and not a pseudo-Bourbon who pretends that he lives in a world that no longer exists (like the service club member talking the liturgical language of unbridled competition while functioning smoothly in a world of 'administered prices' and tariff protection).

I have granted, if a little grudgingly, that the Bourbon may serve a valid Christian function, mainly as a check-and-balance to the Jacobin. More often, I think, the Christian will be called to be a Jacobin. He knows that man's powers of reason were given him for a purpose; that his sense of justice was instilled in him to deny him an easy conscience. He knows that man need not be like the beasts of the fields that live by instincts or drives. God has given man within broad limits the chance to reshape society and the natural environment. Man cannot abdicate that responsibility by settling for whatever society just happens to exist at one point in time. He is summoned to dream dreams, dreams informed with as much Christian insight as possible, and then try to make them real. But he will do well to take the Bourbon seriously and listen to him; he should also read the dystopian books I have been discussing. The Bourbon and the dystopian will give him a check-list of things to watch: Have I over-simplified? Am I forgetting the Law of Reverse Effect? Have I taken into account Lord Acton's observation? Am I counting too much on rationality and benevolence? And there are many other questions to answer.

But perhaps it is unfair and unrealistic to expect the utopian dreamer to ask himself all these questions constantly. He properly has eyes of fire; he is an all-outer, an extremist. He cannot be told to pause every moment and footnote his own dreams. The poet cannot be the definitive critic of his own poems.

So, as what I know is an anti-climax, I conclude that the conscientious Christian should in most cases find himself called upon to carry on a dialectic between the Bourbon and the Jacobin in the depths of his own being. There should be a creative civil war; he could not try to impose a peace treaty. He should read both *A Modern Utopia* and *We*, and say "Yes, but" to both of them. He should know that the utopian is right to dream dreams, and the dystopian is right to put them under the microscope.

Such a person is a kind of Churchill or Franklin Roosevelt. He operates within a living tradition that is emotionally close to him. Because he loves it, he wants to improve it. But he is not ready to scrap it and accept another society *in toto* from the drafting board. He has a vision of how the actual society can evolve constantly towards something better while still retaining as much as possible of all that is now good in it. He tolerates and even respects the Bourbon; he challenges the Jacobin. But he takes the Jacobin very seriously for he knows that the latter's dream also comes from a kind of love.

The person with the civil war inside will seem sometimes radical, sometimes conservative, depending on what club the observer belongs to. This was true of the way Roosevelt and Churchill appeared. He will sometimes do radical things for conservative ends. He will remodel whole areas of society to make sure that society can keep its continuity, its sense of tradition, and remain viable. Thus Roosevelt introduced social security and many fiscal controls not in order to destroy free enterprise but to make it tolerable enough to survive.

These are generalities. There may be times when the role of the Bourbon is imperatively necessary; when a reasonably good society is faced by alternative changes, all of them bad. Just before the time of Hitler, Germany may have been such a country. The actual possibilities of change, humanly speaking, were communism and nazism. The Weimar Republic, though no utopia or Christian paradise, was worth defending against the two alternatives.

Certainly, and more often, the times may call for the Jacobin. In many of the emerging countries there can be little realistic talk about preserving or developing an established way of life, when it consists of tribalism, witchcraft, and sometimes cannibalism. To survive in the 20th century and be worth surviving, these countries must create a new way of life. It may be possible to incorporate much of the old, but the new is of necessity likely to dominate. The process involves such prosaic spectacles as planners sitting around a table to allot economic priorities, and even committees at work inventing new words for some local dialect that must be upgraded into a national language. In relatively stable countries it is easy to forget that the Jacobin, the great planner, may be essential for the very survival of nations that are little more than a cluster of tribalisms when 'freedom' suddenly surprises them.

We have now come full circle. I argued earlier that the dystopian writers were latter-day prophets, proclaiming judgement upon mankind if it takes wrong turnings. I now say with equal emphasis that the utopian also fulfils a prophetic purpose. He summons men to good dreams, and the attempt to do something about them. He proclaims that no society is good enough, and that the complexity of society is no excuse for evading the attempt to improve it.

The utopian dream can be shallow, but it need not be. We dare not let it die. I do not think we will. The dialectic must continue. If the utopian is too busy to read the footnotes supplied by the dystopian, that becomes the sober talk of you and me who carry the civil war in our depths. But footnotes are not the heart of any book. Let us read the footnotes well, read, mark and inwardly digest. But then we look again at utopia. We shall have no peace until we incarnate as much of it as we can in brick, stone, laws, customs, and even the free motions of the unplanned heart.

Appendix

Books for further reading

The reader who wishes to explore utopia and dystopia more extensively and deeply will find the following books useful — I can personally vouch, and with gratitude, for that. All of them contain additional titles of primary works.

Amis, Kingsley: *New Maps of Hell: A Survey of Science Fiction* (Harcourt, Brace & Co., New York 1960; Victor Gollancz Ltd., London, 1961).

Bailey, J. O.: *Pilgrims Through Space and Time: Trends and Patterns in Scientific and Utopian Fiction* (Argus Books Inc., New York, 1947).

Berneri, Marie Louise: *Journey Through Utopia* (Routledge & Kegan Paul, London, 1950).

Clarke, I. F.: *The Tale of the Future: A Checklist of satires, ideal states, etc., published in the United Kingdom* 1644–1960 (The Library Association, London, 1961).

Gerber, Richard: *Utopian Fantasy: A Study of English Utopian Fiction since the end of the Nineteenth Century* (Routledge & Kegan Paul Ltd., London, 1955, and Hillary House Inc., New York, 1956).

Gibson, R. W.: *A Preliminary Bibliography of St. Thomas More with a Bibliography of Utopias and Dystopias,* 1500–1750 by R. W. Gibson and J. Max Patrick (Yale University Press, New Haven, Connecticut, 1961).

From Utopia to Nightmare

Hertzler, Joyce Oramel: *The History of Utopian Thought* (The Macmillan Company, New York, 1922; Geo. Allen & Unwin Ltd., London, 1923).

Meyer, Karl E.: *The New America: The Age of the Smooth Deal* (Basic Books Inc., New York, 1961).

Morton, A. L.: *The English Utopia* (Lawrence & Wishart, London, 1952).

Mumford, Lewis: *The Story of Utopias* (Boni & Liveright, New York, 1922: Peter Smith, Gloucester, Mass., 1959; Geo. G. Harrap, London, 1923).

Negley, Glenn & J. Max Patrick: *The Quest for Utopia: An Anthology of Imaginary Societies* (Abelard-Schuman, New York, 1952 and Doubleday, N.Y.).

Russell, Frances Theresa: *Touring Utopia: The Realm of Constructive Humanism* (Dial Press Inc., New York, 1932).

Index

The more important references are given
in **bold face** numerals

Index

Index

Index

Hilton, James, 55.
Hitler, 116, 150, 158; *Mein Kampf*, 121.
Huxley, Aldous, 11, 14, 25–6, 28, 39, 72, **92** ff, 103, 106, 112–3,
   135, 137 ff, 165, 176 n.
Howells, William Dean, 83.
Hudson, W. H., 83.
Hunt, H. L., 14, 176.
Hypnopaedia, 93, 149.

Île de Naudely, 74.
Individual and the State, The, 49, 60, 71, 144, 167.
Individuality, 38, 43, 44, 53, 65, 80, 141–3, 145, 167.
In Memoriam, 19.
Island, 14, 97 n, **137**, 176 n.
Islandia, 55.
It Can't Happen Here, 104.

Karp, David, 114.
Kipling, Rudyard, 61.
Koestler, Arthur, 129, 133, 157.
Kornbluth, C. M., 164.
Krutch, Joseph Wood, **162** n.

Laicus, Philipp, 75.
Last and First Men, 28, 55, 71.
'Law of Reverse Effect, The', 151–2, 156, 157, 169, 180.
Lewis, C. S., 28, 139, 147 n, **163**, 165.
Lewis, Sinclair, 104.
Liberal, The, 129–30, 132–4, 155.
'Life, Liberty and the Pursuit of Welfare', **162** n.
Limanora, 89.
Limbo, 140, **149–50**.
Literacy, 119, 121.
Lobotomy, 102–3, 108, 149, 150, 167.
Looking Backward, 11, **49** ff, 67, 74, 78.
Looking Forward, 75.
Looking Further Backward, 74.
Lord of the Flies, 28.

Index

Lost Horizon, 55.
Love Among the Ruins, **79** ff, 151.

Machines, The, 51, 53, 83, 84, 85, 86, 100–3, 151.
Machine Stops, **83** ff, 90, 140, 151–2, 165.
Marx and Marxists, 24, 51, 56, 116, 124, 131.
Marx, Karl, 41, **129** ff.
Memoirs of the Year Two Thousand Five Hundred, 59.
Mercier, Louis Sébastien, 59.
Michaelis, Richard C., 75.
Miller, Walter M., Jr., 28, 164–5.
Mittelhölzer, Edgar, 58.
Modern Utopia, 11, 25, 39, **52** ff, 64, 70.
More, Thomas, 24–5, 36, **40** ff, 56, 176.
Morris, William, 83.
Mr. East's Experiences in Mr. Bellamy's World, 75.
Mumford, Lewis, 55.

Nabokov, Vladimir, **105–6**.
Nature in Utopias, 29, 139–40.
Nazis and Nazism, 104, 113, 178, 180.
New Atlantis, 18, **46–7**.
News from Nowhere, 83.
Nineteen Eighty-Four, 11, 39, 97–98, **106** ff, 135, 140 ff, 157–8.
Nuclear Weapons Dilemma, The, 158, 159.

Oceana, 48.
One, 114.
Origin of Species, 19–20, 119.
Orwell, George, 11, 39, 97–8, **106** ff, 135, 140 ff, 157–8.
Out of the Silent Planet, 147 n.

Pallen, Condé B., **78–9**.
Pascal, Blaise, 91.
Pessimism, 18, 23, 52.
Planning, 21, 44, 49, 55, 75, 93, 134, 137, 139, 168, 169–70, 174, 176, 177, 178, 179, 181–2.

Index